HACKNEY LIBRARY SERVICES

B

Please return this book to any library in Hackney, on or
before the last date stamped. Fines may be charged if it is late.
Avoid fines by renewing the book (subject to it NOT being reserved).

Call the renewals line on 020 8356 2539 06/13

People who are over 60, under 18 or registered disabled
are not charged fines. 811.008

PJ42014

⊕ Hackney

D0241206

JUBILATION!

poems celebrating 50 years
of Jamaican Independence

Edited by

KWAME DAWES

PEEPAL TREE

First published in Great Britain in 2012
by Peepal Tree Press Ltd
17 King's Avenue
Leeds LS6 1QS
UK

Thanks are due to Justine Henzell
and Chris DeMarco for their help in putting
together this anthology and to
the National Library of Jamaica for their help
in finding the cover photograph.

ISBN 13: 9781845232047

Supported by
ARTS COUNCIL
ENGLAND

DEDICATION

You imagined a nation long before we learnt the dialect of nations,
and often bewildered, vulnerable and alone, you stripped

to your naked self to find a body free of the vestments of our undoing.
We called you mad, ignored your genius, wounded your spirit

and left you to be broken by the elements. In your flawed
music you discovered the vein of genius, something we now

mine for our art, and for this we thank you, makers of first
poems; you tested it all, left us with the charts marking gullies,

sheer drops, fresh creeks, shade trees, and the sweetest fruit
to make us fat, drunk, and full of our delicious awakening.

Give thanks, give thanks.

Remembering

Vera Bell
Louise Bennett
George Campbell
H.D. Carberry
Neville Dawes
Ras Dizzy
Gloria Escoffery
Barbara Ferland
John Figueroa
A.L. Hendriks
Archie Lindo
Thomas McDermott (Tom Redcam)
J.E.C. McFarlane

Claude McKay
Anthony McNeill
Roger Mais
Una Marson
Daisy Myrie
Victor Stafford Reid
W.A. Roberts
Andrew Salkey
Dennis Scott
Philip Sherlock
M.G. Smith
Mikey Smith
Vivian Virtue
Gwyneth Barber Wood

And the many poets whose work has come to shape our idea of the
Jamaica poetic.

CONTENTS

INTRODUCTION

It is only incidental that this anthology of Jamaican poetry is the first to appear in quite a few years. Incidental but fortuitous, because it is an undeniable fact is that we have good reason to celebrate what is becoming quite a remarkable body of poetry being published by Jamaican poets over the past decade. This made putting together the anthology quite easy. I already had a long list of published poets to approach for contributions, and I had an even longer list of emerging poets who are producing work of a high standard that I could invite to submit.

The anthology seemed like a fit way to celebrate the fiftieth anniversary of Jamaican Independence, and regardless of what one may think about Jamaica's challenges today, there is little question that 1962 constituted a tremendous achievement and a notable milestone in the development of what we like to think of as a Jamaican identity. Celebrating the fiftieth anniversary made sense. Doing so with poetry made even better sense.

That original moment, marked by a certain euphoria, brought with it so much promise – more promise than was probably realistic. Mervyn Morris's delicately visioned and deeply ironic summation of that moment in which the celebrants were "too young for disillusion", offers a wry comment on that optimism, which he quickly undermines. From the perspective of a backwards look, all celebration of fifty years is seen as a pretence, a sham, a forced elation. Yet, in a backhanded way, Mervyn Morris does suggest that we have grown up. Now we are old enough for disillusion. It is a useful caution, but, of course, it is not the whole story. Indeed, the poems collected here are not the whole story, but their number, their variety, their ambition, take us closer to at least contemplating a

13

broader sense of the story than we might have in the limits of our own heads.

I had some options about how to tackle this project. I did consider pulling together an anthology of poems published over the past fifty years. The problem with that was that we would have ended up with quite familiar work from the past, especially if these poems were in some way to be celebratory of independence. In the Dedication, we have paid a too brief homage to those Jamaican poets who are no longer alive, on whose shoulders we stand, but I wanted to give Jamaica a collection of the moment, a collection of poems that would be a very contemporary reflection on these fifty years of independence, made with the complexity and reflective wisdom that poetry can bring to any subject when in the right hands.

The challenge, of course, was for the poets. I asked them to send me some work that reflected on the fiftieth anniversary. I asked them, in other words, to write new poems for the anthology. But I really did not hold firmly to that notion (and numerate readers will also note that there is a properly Jamaican approach to the elasticity of numbers – this is fifty an' a brawta). The reason for this flexibility was my awareness that some poets had already started to think about this occasion and had written work responding to it, and that there existed poems fairly recently published that would that were a wonderful fit for the collection.

As a result, we have an anthology of mostly new poems, and a number of slightly more familiar poems that manage to resonate beautifully with the core themes of Jubilation! But what appeals to me most about this anthology is that it speaks beautifully to what is happening with Jamaican poetry today – so many poets with recent books of poetry, so many active and performing artists, so many writers working out of our multiple traditions to create a varied and sophisticated sense of what it means to be Jamaican and a poet today.

These are not poems of casual and predictable celebration. These are not poems of superficial elation. These are not poems for greeting cards and tourist brochures, or the political platform. Instead they are poems that take risks, that challenge our sense of self, that are not reluctant to show us our ugliness and our beauty, that willingly dance between public declaration and deeply lyrical reflection. In other words, these are poems that are asserting their value to us as poems first, and only afterwards attempting to be voices in the business of celebrating our fifty years.

More than anything else, my feelings about the publication of this anthology are those of gratitude. I am extremely grateful for the generosity of each of the poets who have contributed to the anthology and who have done so with enthusiasm and appreciation. I am grateful to Peepal Tree Press for embracing this project without hesitation and for making it such a lovely book. And I am grateful to you, the readers of this anthology for thinking it fit to take a look at what is an important historical marker of our development as a nation.

The greatness of Jamaica lies in its inability to see itself as small. It is also one of our failings, but I suspect that the benefits that accrue from this piece of madness far outweigh the negatives. It is this elegant arrogance that has somehow allowed us to engage the world with complete confidence and the assurance that what we have to offer is valuable and meaningful. I have always credited reggae music for teaching me this aspect of the Jamaican sensibility that clearly existed long before Toots gave this name to our music. It is out of this confidence that I recommend this collection to you. I say to you that you will find here some remarkable gems, poems that will reward reading and rereading.

Kwame Dawes

OPAL PALMER ADISA

FIRE EATING TRADITION

her great grandfather
was a fire eater
from slavery days
served under nanny
spewing fires
to confuse
the maroons' tracks

her father ate fire
entertained the planters
with his skills
burned down fields
and secured land for himself
he showed her
how to hold hot coal
in her fisted palm
to cure illness

she taught herself
how to eat fire
cool the outer rims
of its orange blaze
take it slowly
into her mouth
then gulp it down
allowing it to spread
in her stomach
she had her first
vision then
saw people waving
black yellow and green
coloured flags in the streets

she didn't know
sixteen years later
in 1962 that would
be independence day

after that
she pondered fire
solicited it
set bushes   sheds
fields ablaze
so she could
skip through it
wear it next
to her skin
and get lost in its
searing blue flames

LILLIAN ALLEN

JAMAICA – I REMEMBER

Sunday evening breeze
Rice an' peas, roast pork and chicken curry
We change from our Sunday-school best
Frilled socks turned so delicately down
Bata cha-cha-cha soulfully brushed to sparkle
The canvas' perfect white
Grinning in the Sunday evening light

We pack up a canteen Thermos
Four medium-sized tin can hooked together
Swing pon each other like a Jacob's ladder
Parboiled an' red beans, chicken-back swimming in yellow grease
Okra, ground provisions
Dinner for granny-auntie-cousin Lovie-Hilda
Down the lane beside Phillippo Baptist Church
French Street corner Spanish Town
Close to Russian shop 'cross from the Chineyman store
Where the East Indian family grows calaloo next door

So abundant tall the guinip tree shadows
Ever blooming limes and a small guava grove
A banging broken wooden gate where the cistern hides
Its pipe drip   drips   drips   dripping
No matter how hard you tighten
The trick – lock it off slight, just right, slow down, quiet
Tip away   sh – ssh – ssshhh
Or else it pours again to dance brushed-green
Slime oh so lazily on the iron grey of the cistern's concrete

And we children, one by one get out hugs
For granny-auntie-cousin Lovie-Hilda
Half blind, lovesome, a no-toothed smile

Soft wrinkles jiggle and ripples sparked to laughter
How granny-auntie-cousin Lovie-Hilda got her name
I couldn't say, but it seems to have spurted with her age

We light up her day, her very existence
We think her Gran Aunt with a proper G
Our Granny-Auntie-Cousin-Lovie-Hilda
Not connected by blood or marriage
Or relatives in common
She was only a woman who way back when
A child in my grandmother's childhood
made blood by passing time.

EDWARD BAUGH

YABBA

From Twi *ayawá*, an earthen vessel,
dish, bowl, larder, cooking-pot,
a plain, useful object, pleasing
to handle, contentment to the eye.
A mug's comfortable, no-nonsense *there-ness*,
the whimsy of a vase, wide rim-sweep
of a dish, shapes spawned and spun
from his conjurer's hands, startle of turquoise
against earth-brown, deep forest green –
yabba and monkey jar turn fine art
and Ma Lou protégé, the "yabba man",
is master potter, maker, craftsman!
High cheekbones' ebony glaze,
forehead etched with wisdom lines,
slant-steady, patient eyes
by turns frolicsome and austere,
his thumbs like spatulas poised –
he's folded in earth now, but his fingers
feel the wet and cling of clay.

RECIPE

For your grandmother

That time of the year when the days are shorter, darker
and cooler, when the poinsettia, fire plant,
its leaves incredibly red, these leaves
surrounding and protecting
the less conspicuous flower,
was when my grandmother's brick oven
became more active than usual.
As grandmother prepared for that day –
glorious is what she called it,
all of us children dressed in white,
in observance of the birth of her lord and saviour.

*

The year I turned ten I started growing into my father's
long arms and legs, his light eyes, his burnished
complexion. I awoke
one morning to an ache in my stomach,
a spot darkening my underwear.
That Christmas, Grandmother called me into her kitchen –
walls blackened by soot,
well-scrubbed silver pots dangling from the roof,
constant smell of pine and hickory.

She handed me, as an early present, a simple
white cotton apron she had stayed up all night,

by the light of the kerosene lamp, to make.

As I placed the apron over my head she began speaking to me,
as she had spoken to my mother and all my aunts –
as my great grandmother had spoken to her and all her sisters:

"Here in Jamaica, there is never the dream of a white Christmas
therefore, the pudding is not served hot.
Housewives make one mixture: bake a portion for the cake,
steam the remainder for the pudding.
Raisins, currants, and stoned prunes
should have been soaking for months
in real Jamaican rum cut by port wine.
Spice may be added –
vanilla and almond flavouring –
but this is not a *must*.
Fruits *must* be soaked in a glass jar
with a tight-fitting lid; avoid using
plastic containers.
And," she paused, before continuing,

"Always measure what you do."

As I stood in the kitchen that first time
doing what I knew I would be doing all my life,
surrounded by the ambiguities of my childhood –
a father long gone, a mother
unavailable to me – I could feel my grandmother
rise to take up space in me, and I knew
she was giving me something to take out
into the world: something I would pass on.

JEAN "BINTA" BREEZE

THIRD WORLD GIRL

I'm a third world girl
uncut diamond
unfound pearl
wakened from my dreaming
far too early for my years
filled with stories
yet untold
young, unknowing
born too old

just yesterday
childishly
I peeped at you through bushes
while you browned on my beach
and swam out of reach of my reality

I was held out by the fences round my shores
my water was locked off while you showered
while you ordered extra ice, my sweat just poured
your path was lit up
while I struggled in the dark
I worked with machete through the jungle
while you strolled through a park

now neatly groomed
I serve you cake and tea

I'm a third world girl
when you brought me to your world
you said you educated me
you said I brought no traditions, no history
no culture, no religion, no language with me

you admitted I could sing and dance
but without logic so you couldn't take the chance
to empower me with managing the money
you wanted me to stay the child
wide eyed and sometimes wild
but always weak emotionally

I'm a third world girl
you can't love me cause
you own me
cause your dollar buys my story
and my paradise is merely your hotel

I'm a third world girl
caught in economic hell
cause you've stolen all my treasures
to build your ivory towers
where I am now housekeeper
and my man is in your cell
all you know is that I clean so well
and if you notice how my bosom swells
I'll be a whore with pleasures I could sell

no, please don't touch me
don't be tender
can't you see
I daren't surrender
without the sureness of equality
we kissed on Star Trek for the first time
on the screen
had to be under alien spell to get it seen
our men, your women made themselves a pleasant scene
but I remain the hairy jungle queen
unless I shave and straighten on the catwalk, tall and thin
this third world girl has grown to women
proud in shape and hair and skin

she's not seeking your attention
but if conversation should begin
drop your guilt trip in the nearest bin

I'm a third world girl
born to the land
where your flags unfurled
empire's over
but the rape's been done
and the blood has been my story
our meeting needs to face our history
tell the present what's become of you and me
before the future brings the possibility
Love at first sight
only happens to the free.

LLOYD W. BROWN

THE RETURN OF THE NATIVE

The dirt-brown fleece below is the city's welcome carpet
rolled out from the sleek hi-tech of the Pacific Rim
to towering walls and crumbling battlements of ancient granite:
re-entry is a state of motionless suspense high above a vast space
slipping slowly behind the trail of shrieking turbines,
and in the din
Hollywood's megalopolis unfolds on a silent screen
under the open weave of that floating rug inching
ever upwards
at my shrinking feet.
From here suburbia is still America dreaming:
a subdivided, sun-drenched innocence
freckled with baseball diamonds and swimming pools,
and at this safe, unobtrusive distance
every cul-de-sac, carefully designed and artfully identical,
glows in the sickly air with the comfortable pride
of hard-won possession.
But downtown and inner-city are
two words in a divided consciousness,
two worlds in solitary,
parallel universes at the nucleus of the urban mass:
post-modern chic, rocketing to heaven,
explodes under my approach,
collapses and dissolves into a pandemonium of battle-
scarred projects and greasy spoons
flashing past the window in the dying seconds of my
touchdown:
I am fallen from airborne grace,
and the lumbering jetliner, awkwardly earthbound, whines
with my old relief and familiar regrets.

So you come back from foreign then!
Ah' is so you grey-up, grey-up now?
But is where the long beard come from?
M' sister boy-pickney turn ol' ramgoat!
Or is turn you turn Rasta in America?

Transformation is quick and easy – again:
I am just another man of steel-faced aspect
in the funereal frenzy of rush-hour California;
and home is where the nightmares are:
front-lines of graffiti warfare edging closer
to mortgaged dreams of rootless phantoms
transfixed by other kinds of homelessness
on Television America,
ragged, derelict and reproving,
trailed by high-gloss pitchmen
and Jamaican thugs dealing dope and death
in this nation's capital.

      Jamaica mash up, boy!
      So-so bad min' and so-so bad mout'.
      An' they will eat out you' eye:
      Politician fool you,
      Lawyerman t'ief you,
      Gunman shoot you,
      An' fam'ly bury you 'live!

My plot is manicured suburban green
in a uniform mass of infinite solitudes,
upscale from the abandoned graveyard of
childhood's tropical playground,
where iron missionaries of deathless will
crumbled to dust under my unthinking feet
in weed-choked shadows of church and empire:
I have arrived
at the dead-end of exile in Everyman's El Dorado –

an easy forgetfulness beggars the good life,
upward mobility is a giddy soaring from
the frozen void of inner space,
and now my ragged beginnings are another's
instant paradise of rented beach boys
and packaged oblivion.

> Touris' down here like peas, pupa!
> Naked woman cover Negril to rahtid 'til
> you can' see san'.
> An', when they shake they behin' to the reggae
> you think is ol' drawers on clothesline
> in a breeze-blow!
> An', the rent-a-dread boy swarm 'roun' them
> like when kling-kling after ripe guava.
> You all gone a stranger yard,
> an' now stranger stretch out in you' bed.
> This place hard as iron, boy,
> but it sweet-sweet like rudeness.
> You can keep to foreign:
> I belong to here –
> Here belong to me.

My belonging is yesterday's faint memory
mocked by the timeless strength of an old man
grounded firmly in place against creeping odds:
in that rock hard presence fancy's roots become dried petals,
brittle fantasies between the covers of a cloth-bound sentimentality;
and in that torrent of cascading metaphors
my bookman's dialect is a drenched silence.
Only the ritual of return remains real and enduring –
another Flying Dutchman's eternal rite of passage,
or the swallows' annual homecoming at Capistrano,
where Rumour swears that they touch down from local hideaways,
for curtain-calls that feed the terrible craving of a ravenous legend.

FRANCES COKE

STILL I SEE

1
Out from the Cave of Emergence
She came, framed in lignum vitae.
Awash with the rivers and springs
that named her, she suffered the rape
of strangers. Lighting their way
with shafts of her sunlight baking
their skins to a gilded bronze,
She fed them the juice
of dry coconuts, slaked the thirst of her rapists,
stirred their insatiable loins.

2
Five hundred years gone –
her mountains grown beyond themselves,
he fluttered the red-white-and-blue to the ground
and hoisted the black-green-and-gold
in the trail of a hesitant midnight wind.
Still I see the charcoal sheen of his face,
the jaw's straight line, the shoulders angled,
a nuance of hope in his eyes.
Miss Olive blew out one candle,
took to the streets in her calico
and danced the soles off her brand new shoes.

3
Five decades gone –
zinc walls wear thin, circles of rust
widening where nails used to be.
Fierce messages shaded in orange and green
echo despair and hate.
Today, the distance from ghettoes to hills

is too small – the path strewn with ramshackle.
The mountainsides parched, the rivers grown dry,
mansions reek with the smell of the dead.
Then, in a hush, they fall to the ground
on their knees. Lips part,
whispering urgent pleas to their gods
to rescue the land estranged from herself
and bring back the season of peace.

4
At the end of the alley down to the sea
at the back of Galina's shoulder, a boom box
roars in the morning sun. Miss Olive stoops
in a starapple shade at the side
of her four-by-five yard, snatching at
nut grass and weeds choking her pink hibiscus.
She straightens her back,
raises her eyes to the sky;
not a weed left in sight.

MEL COOKE

COUNTRY COME A TOWN

I come a town pon a truck

I did come before
in a 72 Dodge Avenger
license FM 1004
in a blue Lancer
wid UNICEF pon de door
in a Mini Clubman
whe seat four
carry five
plus coconut pon de floor

An when all a dem bruck dung
an drag me family from miggle class
into landed poor
I tek bus

But de las' time I come a town
afta dem bruck eena de house
mi faada bruck him back pon farm work
an me connection
wid him lan bruck

I come a town pon a truck

I leave the land pon a Leyland
It funny how tree generation
pack up inna some cubic foot a sheet iron
whe usually carry san'

Me grandparents' mahogany four-poster
to the Courts sofa – whe done pay fa

32

I lef Wilmington
pass true Stanton
drop out a Morant Bay
which part I used to walk to my faada
backa Uncle Sydney hardware counta
from Lyssons school every day

Is like I a go Munro one more time
wid a different view from de truck back
higha, but lowa

Like every immigrant me plan fe go back
but is like me get stuck
renting one address to de nex'
every time I haffi lif de wardrobe I vex

When I come a town pon a truck

CHRISTINE CRAIG

MY SON

My boy is on the brink of disaster
prey to violent media images
nasty, noisy music, claws snatching
and pulling him out to the streets
the compulsions, the doors opening
and closing quietly at night
the lies, the excuses
the mutters and slouches
the friends who won't
look you in the eyes
the schoolwork not done
and the mother
tense, red-eyed,
talking, pleading, shouting
tears, prayers.

Her boy is falling, but she can't let him go.
She won't let him go.
I breathed with his first breath
I laughed with his first smile
he is the brightest and best
my brilliant morning star.

The mother spread her net
called out the prayer warriors
those stalwart women who have
come through tumult and adversity.
Those grey-haired men, some who have
walked the same path themselves, others
always steady in their faith. She called them all
called them out and they too spread their nets.

There is no strength like the might
of Jamaican women – can't bend it, break it
or throw it in the fire! There's no fight
like the fight of Jamaican men
who have chosen to walk in the light.

It took weeks, it took months but they stood firm.
One night, it all roared and crashed in his brain
he fell, struggling, fighting the pain in his heart
in his head, the agony streaming
in his blood, till he felt the power
found the strength to save his life.

The mother smiles all day
love and joy bright in her eyes.
Give thanks my friends!
My boy was on the brink of disaster
but we wouldn't, we couldn't
we didn't let him go.

KWAME DAWES

IMPOSSIBLE FLYING

"Palms of Victory/ Deliverance is here!"
1980 Jamaica Labour Party campaign song

1

On Kingston's flat worn earth,
everything is hard as glass.
The sun smashes into the city – no breath,
no wind, just the engulfing, asthmatic noonday.

We move with the slow preservation
of people saving their strength
for a harsher time. 1980:
this land has bled – so many betrayals –
and the indiscriminate blooding of hope
has left us quivering, pale,
void, the collapsed possibilities
causing us to limp. We are a country
on the edge of the manic euphoria
of a new decade: Reagan's nodding
grin ripples across the basin's
surface. We dare to dream
that in the spin and tongues of Kapo
perhaps we too will fly this time,
will lift ourselves from the slough
of that dream-maker's decade –
the '70s when we learned things only
before suspected: our capacity for blood,
our ability to walk through a shattered
city, picking our routine way to work
each morning. We are so used now to the ruins,
perhaps more than that, perhaps to wearing

our sackcloth and ash as signs of our
hope, the vanity of survival.

In that decade when a locksman
could prance the streets with a silver
magic trail in his wake, how we fought
to be poor, to be sufferers, to say
Looking at you the better one; how
we cultivated our burden-bearing,
white-squall, hungry belly,
burlap-wearing, Cariba-suited
socialist dream; how reggae
with its staple of faith, fame
and fortune spoke its revelation
from the speakers of souped-up
BMWs. Gone now, all gone.

We have thrown off that dead skin now;
and the fleets of squat Ladas
are rusting, O Havana.
We've grown too cynical for such austerity
or perhaps we did not suffer enough.
So on such blank and startled days, we dream
of flight. How we hope: *Dance!*
Dance, damn it! Dance, damn it! Be happy!
Our apocalypse echoes on the sound system
and we dance. These laws, these new laws,
these palm leaves, these clamouring bells,
so desperate for deliverance,
this insipid green in the future, and we all
stare at the unflinching sky
and will our hearts to fly.

2

And how you ran, sprinting
down Carlisle Avenue,
your face set against the bare wind;

you were spreading your arms
undulating in complete faith
in the wind's lift,

the physics of the updraft;
past the low fences,
the skittish yelping dogs,

the streaks of telephone wires,
the hibiscus hedges
a blur of green and pink

and smudged off-white;
and me calling you,
trying hard to bring you back;

me catching up,
behind you now, our heat,
our panting, the slap of bare feet

on the soft asphalt;
and I reached for you,
held you by the waist,

drawing you down;
and it felt in that instant
not like a shattering of faith

but a struggle to keep
you home, for each tendon
of your body throbbed

with the lightness of a body
prepared for flight.
And my betrayal was to become

the burden,
the anchor you had
for years longed to shake off.

Stillness, the gaping crowd
staring at this sudden accident:
two men in a heap

of twisted limbs
on the road;
you saying, *This time, this time,*

this time if you had let me,
it would have happened.
I too felt the vanity

of our beaching.
The bells shimmered;
the dispatches were in:

No one
was flying
no more.

A COMPLEX AGELESS LONGING

For Neville Dawes

The cassia flowers bloom a startling yellow
in the branches' shelter; every blue light
turns a mellow breath and brown ska thumps
where Kingston is cooler, deep in the shade.
Imagine a prophet stepping out of tendril
roots and dangling flowers like fruit;
imagine her expanding her arms
and speaking through lips lined white
with fasting, imagine this as a way
to understand the hills, the way they purple,
then blue to something charcoal and old
when the mist falls on them: then
you will have understood the calculation
of faith, not doctrine. Under the soft
topography of fluid light, a white-
dressed prophet, her body dark
and knotted, her breasts like stones
against the stiff fabric of her garment,
is the icon of an island. The tabernacle
warns us to listen and do, tells us
that all seed planted and watered,
though fresh, will die in this barren ground
where stones multiply and shards
of smashed bottles glint in the bare
light. Prodigy saints – that coterie
of precocious, tongue-speaking infants –
step out of the shelter of the cassia
full-grown, their eyes hungry
for the light on the hills.
Despite this we find poems
written by an apostate father full
of gospel and faith. Now his death
is a mystery. Perhaps the half

has not yet been told. Perhaps we may
speak on the other side, the things
of soft soil, quiet hills and the loam
of old villagers, that churchgoing
tribe of black folks who move at dawn
like gashes of white against the gloom.

UPON OUR 14TH ANNIVERSARY
for Lorna

We drive through the irregular curves and dips
of Kingston's suburbs, deep craters, cluttered gullies
cutting through roads. Adjoa's tiny car is a shelter
of laughter and the making of nostalgia. We know
people die on these streets all the time – but tonight
we are able to forget. We spend thirty minutes
making nonsense of the rituals of violence,
and for a day we recall the paths of our love,
the brick porch where I sang songs into the night,
the hall's spine I walked up to see you in the powder-
blue frock, your smile – the first hit of a chronic
addiction I still tremble for all these years later.
Sometimes home is a poem of lament, but tonight
we see Kingston as a freshly painted world of chaos,
a kind of giddy playground. So that after the steamed
snapper and gummy bammy, the coconut water
and guava-pineapple juice at the Fish Place
on the decent end of Constant Spring Road,
Adjoa's car is filled with our children so loud
with playground laughter and the sweetness
of children teetering on the edge of rudeness,
singing Julio Iglesias and Simon and Garfunkel.
We marvel at Kekeli's deep baritone –
him just barely eleven – holding on to each
note's curve as he anchors Paul Simon's thin voice
until we arrive safely, feeling groovy, at West Road.
We sit in the dark until the last guitar strum
and our voices have settled into the hum of joy:
and I understand, again, why I love you, I love us.

RICHARD "DINGO" DINGWALL

IN THIRD WORLD SHADE

Everything is slow here, I feel is di heat.
Slow like salt dissolving canons on Royal forts,
canons now mockingly flawed in orientation.
Slow,
like the languid jelly trees siphoning Portland loam.
Painfully slow...
like when justice not coming.
There is problem inherent in "no problem".
When estates merge to form island, yu always aware yu living on
        somebody property.
Dissent, understandably tempered by the involuntary muscle
        that is memory,
demands don't gush from thank-you mouths.
Time jus nuh ina no rush here;
I still feel is di heat.
But we,
generation vex,
intolerant of kerchief-bosomed vestiges,
refusing to celebrate meagre servings of cerasee pulp,
we claim time.
But maybe clock don't have second-hand memory like we.
Seen osnaburg backs now reclined in boardroom chairs and
        chimed progress,
live fi si breadfruit find countenance,
and witnessed reduced interest by commercial banks in the complexion
        of tellers,
clock jus a gwaan tek it own time.
And in the green-stained, oxygenated hills of Coka district,
        Maggoty's balcony,
overlooking acres and acres of unsweet history,
country people still sit for hours on verandahs and stare,
jus stare...
Contentedly, unaffectedly
one hour behind New York.

43

MARCIA DOUGLAS

VOICE LESSON FROM THE UNLEASHED WOMAN'S UNABRIDGED DICTIONARY

Cimarrón.
Cimarrón.
Remember to roll the r's.
(Think of the sound of galloping mustangs on a Nevada plain)
Cimarrón
(or the pound of buffalo hoofs)
Cimarrón
(or your grandma's mules broken loose last year.)

Maroon.
Maroon.
Breathe in deep,
say it like a warrior hurling her spear through the air.
Maroon
(Now think of bloodhounds, armed men at your heels)
Maroon
(or Nanny's boiling cauldron set to catch them)
Maroon
(or women wearing the teeth of white soldiers around their ankles.)

Maroon.
Pronounce the "a" soft like the "a" in "alone".
That's right,
marooned.
(Imagine dangling from an orange tree, blindfolded –
stockings from someone's clothesline noosed around your neck)
Marooned.
(or the one dollar to your name,
the eviction notice taped to the door)
Marooned.
(think of a cold, soundproof room.)

Maroon.
Say it slow like a rich, full thing to the mouth —
Maroon
(Remember yourself, six years old, talking sassy
                    in your mother's dark lipstick)
Maroon
(or Zora's lips mouthing *"just watch me,"*
                    her felt hat tilted to the side of her head)
Maroon
(or all those women's mouths in Ebenezer choir, *Free at Last*,
singing for the fire locked up in their bones.)

Here's your chance now,
follow the instinct of your tongue
and say it your way,
Maroon.
Put on that hat you wear when you're all stirred up and need
                    to have a word or two.
Hurl your spear if you like,
or change the accent on the "a" —
perhaps something wide, free like the "a" in gallop —
Maroon!
(Hear the call of an old abeng?)
Maroon!
Say it
Say it rich
Say it full
(The twitch near your ear is only the remembrance of thunder.)
But listen.
Listen for the feet of summer rain behind you.
Say it strong
Say it *now*
Break loose speckled horse,
and take yourself back.

THE GIFT OF TONGUES

When Daddy got baptised in Yallahs River,
he rose up speaking –
Oh-shali-waa-shali-mahi-wa.
His eyes shut tight as a newborn's,
someone wrapped him in a white sheet
and led him out of the water.
The brethren clapping and singing redemption,
the white-wings flew
Mahi-shali-ma
from tree to tree along the winding bank.
Daddy would never be the same –
he was filled,
the tongues always waiting to erupt from his lips,
Oh-shali-waa-shali-mahi-wa.
Week after week, he had knelt at the altar,
his mouth open,
waiting to be anointed Child of God.
Now, at Wednesday night prayer meetings,
Daddy flung up his arms
Oh-shali-waa
in the air
his feet keeping time on the red tile floor.
Surely, he had the gift of tongues;
Daddy wouldn't pretend,
would he?

Years have passed now, and I understand:
Daddy spoke for the feeling, not just the language.
It's like after a woman's been in labour for days,
and then a small body is pushed from between her legs,
Oh, shali.

Or like after you've trekked Blue Mountain peak,
so far

so far
so far
and you reach it,
but there are no words to say,
Shali mahi wa.

I picture myself an old woman on a sofa.
Blue light slants through the blinds
and makes horizontal marks like notepaper on the wall.
I fill in the lines:
Oh shali waa,
shali mahi wa.
Shali.
Shali.

MAKESHA EVANS

DIFFERENT REVOLUTIONS

Sunflowers on Spanish Town Road
swashes of blue and yellow
stark against Tarmac arteries
with buildings lining them like plaque.

Greys and browns are everywhere
reflected in sombre faces and dusty feet.
Pigs investigate trash
some distance from the goats,
even they, enterprising.

There are zinc shacks too hot for busyness
so that their people are spat out
to sell bottled water, peppered "swims"
and a ganja-smoking Bob Marley
on a beach towel,
his words, their muted soundtrack:
"It takes a revolution
to make a solution."

And these people are revolving
in their spheres of confluence
arms outstretched to passers-by
not bare but with wares
rubbing bills together
turnin' han' to mek fashion
mickles making muckles
without bloodshed

as if, standing on the roadside,
they signed a treaty that said,
"Sunflowers will thrive here for
our revolutions must be different".

WHERE WE...

We trespass into the waters
right where
the sign says we should not
where the tiny whitecaps
betray currents that could draw us down
where floating sediment paints our skin
where protozoa disperse or cling
their laziness interrupted
where submerged we cannot stand
but can feel
where in washing each other
we become dirtier still,
and where, when we emerge –
our smiles as wide as Kingston Harbour –
the leaves on the coastline
quiver in witness,
their movements like gossip.

DELORES GAUNTLETT

POINCIANA TREE IN BLOOM

I never see the things it cannot do
nor doubt the unspoken will to shoot
for the sky no matter what.
This tree I slow my driving for
already knowing what I'm going to see:
the flaming rush of sunset-orange
astride every branch of its wise old self
that knows the depth of past and present.
I'm tempted to ask it
something human, but I don't.

This is the tree I described in my last letter,
and though you could not guess its name
you understood the ground
from which its tangled roots protrude;
that though its limbs may bend
and its petals fall one by one
you understood it's like seeing time
for what it really is —
the poetry of standing still
where soil and moonlight meet.

TO THE BEAT OF THE TAMBOURINE

She returned to the Pentecostal memory
of redemption songs,
recognized the rhythm of the red tambourine
where soul clapped its hands
to the wonder-working power
of songs that were not her husband's.
She returned to the church he frowned upon,
that same year she was trying to tell him something
she could never talk about with words,
when she whipped up her courage
with the rattle of the red tambourine
and channelled her attention
away from what she had been living for years,
and, with everything she could muster,
transformed in the wake of a joyful noise.

SUSAN GOFFE

STILL WE SING

from a hill above the stadium
we watched the lights go down

seeds of fear already planted
in my grandma's heart
kept us away that night

the lights came on again
then fireworks greeted independence

such hope

even now, such hope
the country still a bone
that stray-dog leaders grip
in the garbage and gully water
of politics' narrow streets

this independence
one more hill for us to climb
and people still know
that while we sing, we work

LORNA GOODISON

HOPE GARDENS

You write to immortalise the long gone
Sunday afternoons light years away by
route of slow silver chi chi omnibus.

Cross Roads   Old Hope   Hope Road,
you in organdy Sunday-school dress set
to slip off good shoes and socks and

dash across the green in Hope Gardens;
as the military band in zouave uniforms,
sounded brass oom pah pah instruments.

Seated now in a seminar, you're perplexed
as this postcolonial scholar unearths plot
after heinous imperial plot buried behind

our botanical gardens; and you think pity
the people never knew this as we posed
for brownie camera captured photographs

by flowering trees, or, O joy, showed off
in our wedding dandan, by lily pond, lay
down ourselves careless in beds of canna

lilies, lost in daydreams of owning own
places with lawns the square of a kerchief.
We the ignorant, the uneducated, unaware

that the roses we assumed bloomed just
to full eye were representative of English
lady beauty; unenlightened we were, so we

picked them on the sly to give as token
to the love we got lost in the maze with –
quick thief a kiss – and this colonial design

was nowhere in mind or sight; but even if
and so what? As long as they flung wide
those two-leaved wrought-iron double gates

here we would be, gentlemen and ladies all,
human beings come in order to draw strength
for the week from our own Hope Gardens.

OUR BLESSED COUNTRY LADY

From my brown cup freckled
            with white dots
                    I'd sip mint or fevergrass tea,
fresh or sweetened with
spoonful of logwood honey
and I'd watch for our Blessed Country Lady.

She who carried a load
            on her head, usually a pile
                    of the island's crosses
she'd elected to bear
for the ones who could not
carry them themselves.

No matter how my own day
            had been, whether or not
                    a poem came or a painting
or a job to pay the rent,
I'd greet her as she descended
the side of the Mountain.

Shifting those burdens slow so
            dark did not fall all at once,
                    she'd hail me back and say,
"Thanks for the greetings.
I would love to come in
and see what you do today

but I am on haste, for I
            have to take this dirty bundle
                    down to the river and wash

it out to sea; that way
when morning come again
some can start over clean."

CHARLIE CHAPLIN AT GOLDEN CLOUDS

Charlie Chaplin declared Oracabessa
Paradise. One hundred and one years ago
on this day time stood still there for him.

At Golden Clouds he smiled and checked in
for a time, the bag of crosses he'd carried
from childhood; case of abandonment and

want that made him identify with the poor
little man; baggypants, jacket too tight, castoff
shoes so outsized, he wore them right to left;

cane and a bowler hat, wicked man's mock
moustache. Jesus what a job! responsibility
for making this world laugh. Chaplin

looked out silent from his room window
framing the Caribbean sea and saw, rowing
hard, big fishermen who cannot swim.

He went for a walk and watched the banana
man who looked like a tramp, cultivating his
acre of hillside land. The inheritors of earth

about their daily business, not caring about
who the great man was, except to offer him a jelly
coconut – Oracabessa sun can be hot – or, like

the chambermaid, recite a psalm as she turned
down his clean sheets, that he might go to sleep
in peace and rise up come morning rested.

JEAN GOULBOURNE

POLITICIAN

Walking down the grimy flag-lined
street
the known man grins
with yellowing teeth

He is who he is
well-favoured
in spite of greed

He sees the flags
instead of those
who hold them

Legacy is
what he leaves behind
his big belly bouncing
as he strides

Behind his grin
he hides

For whatever happens
when Polly
tickles Cain

In his bed at nights
he knows the
pinch of pain

MILLICENT GRAHAM

GALILEO'S MOTION

Duly, the cotton shapes in the half-light, flittering
like wafers on a path, are men returning
to their deserted stations to
pull the guinea-hen weed's dim root,
as tenderly as cold air pinches the throat,
then revives.

The morning happens on their backs,
a voice hums, barely, to the aimless rail
I hear the trains
are coming back again...
A roller winces, flattening out tar
to pave a thin skin over the old ways.

Past them, three women flee in a car,
flanked by a ribbon of retaining walls
meaning to lasso the Hope
River and wind with the coast –
past black-balding hillsides rid of goats
        past the swinging bridge, now in braces,
            past   stilted houses,
            past   newly silted stops,
                    past the shallows where revivalists
                    often gather on loosening cobbles,
            a run of water breaking at their calves,
            atremble, as wind-shredded palms;
        past the straight road through receding crops –

Three visitors,
        touring what weeds forgot,
feeling the little, shut windows cannot shut:

the stock of air-brushed paradise;
the goat-eyed vendor, the men dry as chalk

who couldn't buck them inside their capsule
here, safe from man's sweet-talk
slow to melt – once polished tongues
turn black from Busta's
sticky molasses-fingers
feeling for wax paper

How did things get this way...
so neatly folded?

Off the road
a marooned museum,
cajoled to touch Ankh,
timid to chance –
they watched, bemused, as children
followed mother into trance

I soon floated
from the burnt weeds
bushed from tombs
and copper boiling pans,
floated to the coastline

to unbaked *grattos*,
and a Folly House
Silently I pined
for the shackled lagoon's lime
to walk backward into a sea
of drifting heads

Then, leaving faces behind
I shot, like medicine
coursing a vein,
willing this hour to yield to the moon.

They joined me, bending like tubes of cane
on a road so broken we drew together afraid
of crossing the field. Here, there were men

fermented in old ways;
we saw one stepping into a barracks
his whole leg hobbled
by a darkness, sleepy as wet-sugar.

My nostrils burned,
even the mind.
The wind loosened its knot
and no weed moved.

We prayed for a highway,
a white line salvation; before
sugar stained the hour's bowl
we fled from those tracks
to ways we knew,
but what we saw
remained.

SALLY HENZELL

MS JUNE

Ms. June
zigzags her way to church
down Cobweb Lane
her hat askew atop
mismatching clothes
eating as she goes
her yesterday's fireside cornmeal mush
flavoured with okra, skellion, garlic, honey
or merely fruit plucked from the dildo cactus
or a mango fallen in her path

She'll carry a bag containing pamphlets, notebooks
writing implements
and bits of paper scribbled over
and in her hair sometimes
a wayside flower
by her side a boy
in need of saving
she'll hum a hymn
her blue eyes darting
from bird to hedgerow
noting lizards ants and clouds forecasting weather
thumbed by hands
a bit black from her cookpot
her floppy Bible
its fine filaments of leaves
poured over, annotated, underlined in red
the passages she knows by heart
held together by faith
the creation story endlessly
discussed, disseminated, explained
to non-believers

like me who cannot fathom
the earth's brief history of 6000 years
and who is carbon-dating to provide dates
adding to those paltry years
the bullshit papist psalter
adding a ton of naughts
greeting sisters
and wearing slips and underthings
that disguise the lingering beauty
that fifty years before
drove sane men maddened by desire
as she daydreamed heaven

ISHION HUTCHINSON

THE ARK BY "SCRATCH"

The genie says build a studio. I build
a studio from ash. I make it out of peril and slum
things. I alone when blood and bullet and all
Christ-fucking-'Merican-dollar politicians talk
the pressure down to nothing, when the equator
confuse and coke bubble on tinfoil to cemented wreath,
I build it, a Congo drum, so hollowed through the future
pyramids up long before CDs spin away roots-men knocking
down by the seaside,
like captives wheeling by the Kebar River. The genie says build
a studio, but don't take any fowl in it, just electric.
So I make it, my echo chamber with shock rooms of rainbow
King Arthur's sword keep in, and one for the Maccabees
alone, for covenant is bond between man and worm.
Next room is Stone Age, after that, Iron, and one I
named Freeze, for too much ice downtown in the brains
of all them crossing Duke Street, holy like parsons.
And in the circuit breaker, the red switch is for death
and the black switch is for death, and the master switch
is black and red, so if US, Russia, China, Israel talk
missiles talk, I talk that switch I call Melchezidek.
I build a closet for the waterfalls. One for the rivers.
Another for oceans. Next for secrets. The genie says build
a studio. I build it without gopher wood. Now, consider
the nest of bees in the cranium of the Gong, consider
the nest of wasps in the heart of the Bush Doctor,
consider the nest of locusts in the gut of the Black Heart Man,
I put them there, and the others that vibrate at the Feast of the Passover
        when the collie weed
is passed over the roast fish and cornbread. I Upsetter, I Django
on the black wax, the Super Ape, E.T., I cleared the wave.

Again, consider the burning bush in the ears of Kalonji
and the burning sword in the mouth of the Fireman and the burning
      pillar in the eyes
of the Gargamel, I put them there, to outlast earth as I navigate on one
of Saturn's ring, I mitred solid shadow setting fire to snow in my ark.
I credit not the genie but the coral rock: I am stone.
I am perfect. Myself is a vanishing conch shell speeding round
a discothèque at the embassy of angels, skeletons ramble to checkout
my creation dub and sex is dub, stripped to the bone, and dub is the heart
breaking the torso to spring, olive-beaked, to be eaten up by sunlight.

PIERRE

It was a boy named Pierre Powell
that was in charge of the atlas

in the cabinet. He also ended days
by shaking the iron bell from Principal

William's window, a work we grudged
him for very little; what cut our cores

twice a week and we had to endure,
was him being summoned to fetch

the key, again from William's office,
to open the varnished box with the world

map, old and laminated, a forbidden
missionary gift trophied besides the Oxford

Set of Mathematical Instruments and other
things seen only by Pierre and Teacher Rose,

who now only nodded to raise him
to his duty. We waited in quiet

his return, Miss Rose all crinkled blouse
and bones with chalk dust in her hair,

did not stir until he was back, panting
at the door. Another diviner nod

and he opened it, unrolled the map expertly,
kneaded out creases and held down edges

for the ruler our eyes followed,
screeching out countries, and etched

in the periphery, a khaki-pillared Pierre,
with a merchant's smile, a fixed blur

in our cry of Algeria, Switzerland, Chile,
soon withered away, and we eyed the field

of dry grass outside, a rusty mule,
statue-frozen in the punishable heat,

Pierre, a phantom sea fraying
over Antarctica, Fiji, Belize, India

of those still in the rote, a liturgy of dunce,
whose one cardinal point, Tropicana

Sugar Estate, so close we could smell the sugar
in process, whistled its shift change,

and terminated Geography. As if punched
from dream, those of us gazers, spared the map

rolling-up and cabinet-locking ceremony,
saw him, with a cord-strung key, an earnest air

bearing him away in a portal of sunlight.
He was absent, the week before summer,

and when Miss Rose, in rare fashion,
inquired, a girl said he had gone back home.

"Home," Miss Rose sounded the strange word.
"Home," the girl echoed and added, "he from Cayman,

Miss, or Canada, somewhere with a C."
We turned to Miss Rose to clarify Canada

~~or Cayman, this elsewhere C curdled~~
to snow in our minds, foreign always spectral,

but she pointed anonymously a crooked
finger and said, "Run to the principal

for the key." The whole class scattered, paid
no heed that not a single one was ordained.

Dusk light, a pair of goats clambers up the hill, their cries soft, almost invisible, suggesting a body where there is none, a living creature with a spirit in a cold cell, lying on newspapers on the former burden of unknown men, music glitters in his ears, and though he must not hope, it is there within the starved place in his chest, it flares memory and sunlight, shadows trawl the sand, a child sleeps by the surf's roar churning like the watcher's father clearing his throat at daybreak before cycling off into the fern path, still wet, for work, and the child shifts to the grove of unripe sea pears no ant nest thrives in, and he feels he must speak his presence, the blood's weight to this land water scrapes away, foam reaching for the child, now a log, brown and dry, suggesting a body where there is none, he stands unrevealed, the slate voice of return sticking like ash in his throat's bobbing urn.

*

By now the pouis of Mona are in full bloom, a crimson plain covering the former slave plantation, an old general buckling his uniform in the morning, looks out a window, does not see the Empire's flailing light and could not have foreseen his subjects, unburdened, passing underneath the aqueducts near the library and theatre, into exam rooms, pouis' scents furious, in their gossips cut short when the electric bell shrieks them to attention, and they consider, "the commonwealth on an even beam", the invigilator's clock's ticking, the sun inching another digit, and another.

*

Months after the invasion, a new market is being opened where the old one was flattened by fire, the garbage is elsewhere, even the ribbed mongrels are absent, they were gone before the army bull-dozed the carapaces of burnt-out cars, fridges, gas cylinders, and made a balm-yard clearing blood had to have run for, and not only blood, for there is no blood in the lime-scoured stalls, but the rumour that the *man*, the dreaded gorgon, don of all dons, the president-minister-chief, has been taken ("by 'copter, boss") to either America or hell, but that is just flatulence from uptown, for in the real streets, behind barb-wired territories, concrete walls consecrated by bullets, it is something else, a whole other story at lights out, the graphite, curfewed moonlight lapsing across the riddled shell buildings, blank windows gape at tankers sleeping in an oases of splinters like maimed sphinxes; is something else, is "him still here, you know," meaning, he will always be here.

*

I must not be too surprised at the rain while writing to you, crisply departed, for no matter how far I have moved away, this always reins me in, the sight of rain and sunlight together, childhood's axle-joy, back-spinning fast downhill after stuffing ourselves with my granny's cakes and ginger beer, and you, ever the lithe-foot playfield king, always ahead, so far ahead, a cloud has eaten your voice and me your dust; yes, you weigh heavily on me, friend, who no longer knows the way to die.

*

"And there was no more sea," the Levant writes in his logbook, undoubtedly stealing from the Book of Revelation, everything recedes like a scroll, and I have forgotten the acacias' noise when you walk under them towards the bare beach, these things in my head: "and for the soul if it is to know itself it is into a soul that it must look" and "the Aegean flower with corpses", October, inconsolable, the asphalt bordering the sea-grass, warm and silver in the blazing afternoon so I know I am alive, and you aren't, and no matter how sure I am that it is going to be there, even after a new heaven and a new earth, once I have crossed the crest by the grove of sea pears and I face it, the hot, moving zinc, our sea, "where I left you thinking I would return", I weep.

DANIELLE JENNINGS

MANGO TIME

The mangoes in my backyard
burst forth as blessings; only
this year, I packed them religiously,
saying to the hands I gave,
this is of my flesh. I won't let her
leave me.

She loved them, especially Rawbin,
as she said in her deep, warm gurgle.
We don't have a Robin mango tree, Ma.
But here's a Julie. Six of them on the
tree for the first time ever... you know
the Blackie? And you had a little bit?
It bear and bear and bear so till this year.
You had to leave for the red dirt to bleed?

She used to sit under the mango tree in country,
and read book all day, a crocus bag of mango to
eat, while my great-grandmother hurled wutliss
gyal never come to nothing through the air, like
a stuffed Mello-Juice box in a Dandy Shandy final ten.
My great-grandfather was already dead, and now
all she had was Vin and this likkle girl inside.
She would sleep sometimes, the breeze cool
and the grass nectary. Dreaming escape.

And the likkle baby come and the granny,
she love her so till. And dem grow close you know.
Like how granny always close to dem granpickney.
Mi granny sen fi har daughter an country
exchange fi Orange Street, Cling Cling Avenue
an Boobie Drive. An Vin look farm work

and nuh come back. Mi granny daughter,
work and work and work, but she cyaa
replace her father. She find my father,
and start dream escape.

And now the mango dem a bear and mi cyaa
eat none wid mi granny. And mi nuh have nobody.
Mi will pick a Julie though. And drill inna mi head,
Yuh granny still deh ya.

LINTON KWESI JOHNSON

REGGAE FE DADA

galang dada
galang gwaan yaw sah
yu nevvah ad noh life fi live
jus di wan life fi give
yu did yu time pan ert
yu nevah get yu jus dizert
galang goh smile inna di sun
galang goh satta inna di palace af peace

o di waatah
it soh deep
di waatah
it soh daak
an it full a hawbah shaak

di lan is like a rack
slowly shattahrin to san
sinkin in a sea af calamity
where fear breed shadows
dat lurks in di daak
where people fraid fi waak
fraid fi tink fraid fi taak
where di present is haunted by di paas

a deh soh mi bawn
get fi know bout staam
learn fi cling to di dawn
an wen mi hear mi daddy sick
mi quickly pack an tek a trip

mi nevvah have noh time
wen mi reach

fi si noh sunny beach
wen mi reach
jus people a live in shack
people livin back-to-back
mongst cackroach an rat
mongst dirt an dizeez
subjek to terrorist attack
political intrigue
kanstant grief
an noh sign af relief

o di grass
turn brown
soh many trees
cut doun
an di lan is ovahgrown

fram country to toun
is jus tissel an tawn
inna di woun a di poor
is a miracle ow dem endure

di pain nite an day
di stench af decay
di glarin sights
di guarded affluence
di arrogant vices
cole eyes af kantemp
di mackin symbals af independence

a deh soh mi bawn
get fi know bout staam
learn fi cling to di dawn
an wen di news reach mi
seh mi wan daddy ded
mi ketch a plane quick

an wen mi reach mi sunny isle
it woz di same ole style
di money well dry
di bullits dem a fly
plenty innocent a die
many rivahs run dry
ganja planes flyin high
di poor man im a try
yu tink a lickle try im try
holdin awn bye an bye
wen a dallah cyaan buy
a lickle dinnah fi a fly

galang dada
galang gwaan yaw sah
yu nevvah ad noh life fi live
jus di wan life fi give
yu did yu time pan ert
yu nevvah get yu jus dizert
galang goh smile inna di sun
galang goh satta inna di palace af peace

mi know yu couldn't tek it dada
di anguish an di pain
di suffahrin di prablems di strain
di strugglin in vain
fi mek two ens meet
soh dat dem pickney coulda get
a lickle someting fi eat
fi put cloaz pan dem back
fi put shoes pan dem feet
wen a dallah cyaan buy
a lickle dinnah fi a fly

mi know yu try dada
yu fite a good fite

but di dice dem did loaded
an di card pack fix
yet still yu reach fifty-six
before yu lose yu leg wicket
"a noh yu bawn grung here"
soh wi bury yu a Stranger's Burying Groun
near to mhum an cousin Daris
nat far fram di quarry
doun a August Town

EVAN JONES

SELF-GOVERNMENT

In the old days
It wasn't our fault
A barefoot black man with yaws
Foot dragging in the gravel
Or young child with a tin of water
Balanced on her head
A madman babbling behind bars
Or woman smiling without teeth...

It was their fault
The ones from overseas
The sweaty ones, the ones with red faces
Passing by in dusty motor cars

It was their fault; they conquered us
Transported us, raped us

When we complained
As Sharp and Bogle did
They killed us.

Now it is our fault
Our fault the maggot slums
The hunger and the drugs
Our fault the murder rate
And the small child in rags
Barefoot on the burning road

Our fault unless you blame
Wall Street, the Kremlin
And the Vatican, Satan's triumvirate.

Meanwhile, the green lizard
Still genuflects in prayer
And the mongoose crosses the road.

THE LAMENT OF THE BANANA MAN

Gal, I'm tellin' you; I'm tired for true,
Tired of Englan', tired of you.
But I can' go back to Jamaica now…

I'm here in Englan', I'm drawing pay,
I go to de underground every day –
Eight hours is all, half-hour for lunch,
M' uniform's free, an' m' ticket punch –
Punchin' tickets not hard to do,
When I'm tired o punchin', I let dem through.

I get a paid holiday once a year.
Ol' age an' sickness can' touch me here.

I have a room of m'own, an' an iron bed
Dunlopillo under m'head
A Morphy Richards to warm de air,
A formica table, an easy chair.
I have summer clothes and winter clothes
An' paper kerchiefs to blow my nose.

My yoke is easy, my burden is light
I know a place I can go to, any night.
Dis place Englan'! I'm not complainin'
If it col', it col', if it rainin', it rainin'.
I don' min' if it's mostly night.
Dere's always inside, or de sodium light.
I don' min' white people staring at me
Dey don' want me here? Don't is deir country?
You won' catch me bawlin' any homesick tears
If I don' see Jamaica for a t'ousand years!

…Gal, I'm telln' you, I'm tired fo' true
tired of Englan', tired o' you.
I can' go back to Jamaica now –
But I'd want to die there, anyhow.

JACKIE LAWRENCE

TIGER BABIES

i.
we are tiger babies
you and I
boldness lives here
boldness lives here

ii.
My six-year-old self tells me I am old
My fifty-year-old self tells me I feel thirty

Sages tell me: I am now one year with forty-nine years' experience

I feel a little wear, a little tear in my joints now
after a strain, a sprain, it takes more time to heal

I could wish all dreams blossom in my lifetime,
love come sooner, doubts disappear

I dance with uncertainty everyday,
be grateful, be content

iii.
Anxious people ask: how we gonna work it out?
Faithful ones reply: when one door closes, many more are opened

2000 year old civilizations tell me: I am a toddler, yet to crawl

I see a little crack, a little tear in the dream now
after energy, election and gale-force winds, it takes more time to
          bounce back

I could wish no more sufferation in my lifetime,
love shines daily, doubts disappear

Freedom comes with choice: to stay, to leave
each has its price, its reward

iv.
we are independence babies
you and I
swaddled in black, green and gold
hope lives here
hope lives here
hope lives here

EASTON LEE

HAPPY ANNIVERSARY

Is seventy-five years now wi deh together,
Married for seventy, today is wi anniversary.
No badder ask mi why wi never married before,
Dat a noh your business; you too faas an inquisitive.

Is plenty plenty tings we go through you know
Plenty laughter and happiness
Nuff grief and nuff tears
Nuff nuff eye water flow
Both fi joy and fi sorrow
All these many years.

You see im deh
Ole brute deaf like a rat bat
An miserable caant done
But a so him gimme trouble
Ah so mi love im.

Is a long time now we a love
An fine virtue inna wi one another.
An if me was to ever married again
It would be him same one, no other
For im is mi husband, mi father, mi brother
An mi very bess friend.

Me know some bad minded people
A wonder say
What me see pon im
What him see pon me
Well every nooko have dem sooko
Me an him belongst together
An every hoe have dem stick a bush

An him a fi mi stick
God meck him fi me and me fi him.

An a no really bush me fine him you know.
Meet him one day a come from church
Oh... love at first sight, so dem say
And a didn't have to look no furder.
Through ups an downs, thick an thin
Prosperity and adversity,
Whole heap a botheration
We stick together all these years lovin
Never think of leavin
Never think of divorce or separation
But Lawd...
You know how much time a think bout murder?

ANN-MARGARET LIM

TAINO OF RED HILLS

The story goes: they were blasting the hill
and found you – three Taino skeletons –
mother, father, child, huddled

like a family facing a tsunami;
like a family about to be hacked,
mown down by a fleet
of genocidal conquistadors.

They excavated you, stored you in a museum,
but your lives lived here on this hill
can't be raked away like the leaves
of my Julie mango tree.

When evening comes with the dying sun
I think of your evenings after the pepper pot,
catching the breeze on a hammock.

When the woodpecker pecks some hollow tree
at sunrise, I think of your mornings
of countless birds in these hills
when the hills were young.

When I drive through the short-cuts of the hill,
down to the river, to the sea,
I imagine your journey downhill
to river, to sea for turtles, for fish.

When I look at my dog reddened by the soil
of this hill, I construct a story
of bloodletting.

RAYMOND MAIR

PIANO RECITAL
Claudio Recabarren, March 17, 2011

Now, the left hand
ushers in twilight,
with a love song,
maybe, or just a kiss,
a love once felt,
the wonder
of a cluster of stars.

RACHEL MANLEY

REGARDLESS

All of us,
bruised by our own
degree of caring,
sat at the edge
of your garden

sensed by the watchful
almond tree
a strong nanny
moved little by time

Around the house
the ginger lilies
pulled their oars
against the breeze
and the hills beyond
remained loyal.

Poinsettias still glow
like Christmas decorations
on a January tree

Plumbago blooms
arrive each year
like guests
well-dressed for tea.

BOB MARLEY'S DEAD (FOR DRUM)

The moon is full
heavy yellow
Marley's dead
and there is prophecy

Hallelujah
Jah is singing on the moon
and all our pain
is like the shadow of a branch
across its face;
it's not the King who lives
long live the King
it is the Kingdom lives

My island is a mother
burying wombs
I rise, at my beginning
the squalor
the flower

The moon is dread
she bleeds
Marley's dead
and there is prophecy

The Kingdom lives
a heart of drums
a small town throbs,
we have begun
the phoenix
from a mulch of bones

I rise beyond
a fantasy
I wake
I break faith
with the white dream

The moon is black
my mother sings with me
Oh Marley's dead
and there is prophecy.

MBALA

BIRTHDAY

don't count candle
count heartbeat
measure how much pressure
bill up bill up bill up
over years an decades
don't count candle
count how much fire
pan di hillside
how much joint a bamboo
a bun an buss
how much shat a buss
at ten minutes to midnight
or midday
don't count candle
don't count years
gather fifty julie mango
tun dung yu pot
lock yu door
and don't blow out
di candle dem
it a get dark

SHARA MCCALLUM

ELECTION DAYS, KINGSTON

There are days so long the sun
seems always overhead, a hefted
medallion hanging in the sky.
They sit in the market,
gathering like flies on fruit, linger in dust
kicked up on roads scorched by drought.
They lie on the base of the neck
like beads of sweat stalling on skin.

These are the days in a country's life
when the air is so still
it collects in folds, drapes itself
through the nostrils of young and old;
when the air is weighted with something
approximating hope.

AT THE HANOVER MUSEUM
Lucea, Jamaica, 2000

Once many believed in a common dream
of this island, variegated skins of fruit

arrayed at market. *Every mickle mek a muckle.*
But the land keeps opening to loss –

flame tree seeds shaken loose from limbs,
sifted flour that will not rise into bread.

Stalks of cane grow, unaware of their irony,
scattered across this museum's grounds.

Inside, shackles affixed to cement blocks
have rusted to vermillion, almost beautiful.

Here, the sea breaking against cliffs
is a voice I might mistake for the past.

At the entrance to town, the sea wall stands.
Balanced on the edge of water and land,

children play in the surf. Fishermen,
visible in the distance,

will later bring in the day's catch:
snapper on a string, mackerel, even barracuda.

In a place where wind drags through leaves,
where dusk can rip daylight to shreds,

I emerge, remembering
how to eat sugar cane:

spit out the pulp,
before it grows reedy and bitter in your mouth.

EARL MCKENZIE

NESTING

While thinking of moving
to a quieter house,
I saw a bird building a nest
on the bonka tree
at my back door.

My birdbook said
my new neighbour
was a bananaquit,
a solitary female
building her house of straw.

The nest was on a bunch of green fruits,
against a pattern of palm leaves,
lit by streaks of morning sunlight.

I would not hear from her
the country's violence of noise,
only an occasional "zizizizi",
soft as the flowers.

That evening,
frond and nest
fell to the shrub below;
birds too
suffer their calamities.

But she persisted,
and with the help of headphones,
so did I.

AGAINST LINEARITY

We reject the straight line.

We crowd and push
and use our elbows
at the entrances
of buses, post offices
and movie theatres.

Our motorists break
the unbroken white line
and overtake the overtaker.

A minibus driver
shouts jumbled destinations,
and his route
is a web
of an anarchist spider.

Our rebels idolise Knotty Dread
for knotty is the way
to Jah and Zion.

We fear the straight line
for it is as rigid as death.

Those who know its power
respect its slide-rule
secrets of accomplishment.

Others want to bend it
into trees and rivers
into the crookedness of life.

MARK MCMORRIS

FAREWELL TO CLARENDON

Dear Claude

This is not really a letter to you
a query to a dead man enigma
going away to sea to London Town
Tangiers   Moscow   Harlem
say that today I am writing
instead to a ghost, a sub-text
printed with aura in *Complete
Poems* with *Constab* crèole
sonnets to a cabaret dancer
and America, a violent summer
that catches fire later
Tuskegee   Kansas   Petrograd
what it feels like to be away
where did you go for a decade
circling an empty alphabet
vanished into the sahel, or African
coastal city remote from islands
if an island can be a place
to begin from and not a sea-port
hiatus in the book of passages
to someplace else and greener
whose name defeats the atlas
of stable local habitation
whose name lies on the border
ships are leaving the origin
behind, bound for colder latitudes
this is a secret I want to know
ships are leaving the cradle
you sang songs about in colour
warm December water falls

the basin of mirrors canted
in ochre light, and the jaw
sings poinsettia preludes to
good-bye green fields of my youth

After fifty years our writing
learns the forms you began with
dialect ballads of the folk
memory planted in the country
(culture is an organic metaphor)
and exchanged for Keats's English
the verse of a colonial century
that you mined, when you built
hymns to nostalgia and the Negro
in Babylon, before Babylon was
a watchword of wickedness and sorrow
and being an outcaste yourself
with *arm of steel* to dig a trench
or beat verse into *fighting back*

People make speech from the alphabet
of the sunlight that they know
strings come undone in time
speech changes, purpose holds
the captain spots a lighthouse
to avoid: a storm-beaten coast
what origin is this I mean
for people like us world nomads

Inside a mariner's heart
the rain falls like pollen dust

.   .   .   .   .

And in Moscow, where you met the Soviet poets
what was the meaning of your address

to Trotsky and the world International
(the same song from the labourers)
then along the Volga, underneath
minarets gleaming in winter light
following the stream of the Neva
The pagan day, the holy day for all
to walk the only voice from there
Clarendon   capital May Pen

I saw the house you lived in once
pitched to a hillside, and rubble
mixed with grass were the grave stones
of generations of that farming house
some were there to let me in
some had slipped back into the land
to write their bones into the page
of Charleville the homestead
a garden with small hills, steep
valleys and the mountains
shadowing the elbow of curves
the car follows and the walkers

Strange a Negro who does not box
Shaw said why poetry why not muscle

chatting in the library of English
And yet these are the outcasts of the earth

An in my study I shall view de wul'

The poet in a village, the village
cradled unto itself, and a whole
history with no badge of conquest
a misty heaven with vaguer liberties
to trouble the songs: this witness
says that the village has no boundary

an inner logic spells his breathing
and makes the site, like a deck
of cards fitted to a spiral mandolin

In a locale of meeting and bivouac
time fills the song with mud
it takes forever to speak a word
to think is to invade and retreat
from the *wul'* you made at once
chanting causes like a catapult
of address to an endless sequence
of patrons, expanding gases

and light to the knowable edge
where water falls into black space

(My sounds bounce in the damp)

In a theatre carefully packed
on ice a myriad nothings prosper
and wait for a change of season
mud and countless blisters
that shape the troubadour and the song

.   .   .   .   .

(*50 verses for 50 years*)

As I think o' you again
De mango-tree neat' which we'd stayed

Wake de lion in your veins
Though it be but a fardin' less

Yet still you don't a go   5
Watch de blue banabees

An in my study I shall view de wul'
If you'll only be / Fe me one, Joanie

You should have heard my heart a beat!
You lazy ones can lay down still   10

Messengers I send along
You 'stan', me chil'? I caan' explain it mo'

Seben lovin' ones in need
Sweetly the wesley horn resounds once more

Coursin' t'rough me frame   15
From de top o' Clarendon hill

Forgive me, Jubba, Jubba dear, etc.
In baggy trousies clad

Wid deir younger tender daughters
De harmless tabby o' de house   20

.   .   .   .   .

Assembled from the *Poems*, my role
scribe of the sojourner
peasant who ditched the country
for voyages to waylay himself
discard what he had, and discover
things a land can teach the exile

.   .   .   .   .

The page is ready – the ink, pencil,
and eraser – the light is adequate
tinged with amber from the fire

97

My breath expelled on a mirror of oil
surface and seeing candle
bent in upon itself like a mobile

.   .   .   .   .

(50 verses for 50 years)

Also dismissed ones
Ef we should go aroun' John's shop

He'll carry me 'fo' officer
Ah massa Jesus! in you' love

O comrades, my comrades   25
Our soul jes' like fe you

You have betrayed the blacks maligned the yellow
Of strength, as would a gardener on the flower

Some day you would put forth your arm of steel
And I'm alone, alone once more   30

I have forgot the special, startling season
In every place, however high, they lurk

Seen on a gleaming gold-white day
Where life is fairer, lighter, less demanding

Music that every heart would bless   35
And tugging and tearing without let or pause

But the rare lovely spirits, even mine
Your lustrous-warm eyes are too sadly kind

As well put forth my swarthy arm to stop
My hungry body's burning for a swim   40

.   .   .   .   .

It's time to reconsider the idea
of Paradise. What to say except
saying it makes it be and bulk
large in the concert of empty.

The empty set mimics the content
of desire, making measure, connects
the palm tree of space to the pull
of magnetic winds somewhat angry.

Paradise is a thing to let go.
It is the whisper you dread
of El Dorado hemmed in by jungle
that changes nightly to insomnia.

The long declining of August light
cloudless temperate evenings
of bare shoulders and sandals
these withdraw into talkative symbols.

Though literature goes forward in Paradise
though breathing diaphragms lie there
the Clarendon of your youth is only language
the summer-long noise of the owls.

.   .   .   .   .

(50 verses for 50 years)

With loveliness eternal like a star
And midst the clouds the gold winds heard their words

Of beauty bathe thee from her lofty throne
Of mysteries that seem beyond life's bar

Your monument remains
Their children on suspicion and in fear   45

Now ripples curl where yesterday lay riven
The murmuring of fruit-ripe throats is sweet

Oh we who have sometimes felt as free as air
And are considered by the snobs to reach   50

.   .   .   .   .

Instead of your person, these verses
must dance the part of 50 years
cut loose from the empire you fought
with Eastman, in the *Liberator* days
How Black Sees Green and Red
twilight of empires after the War

.   .   .   .   .

Clarendon exists in the Paradise
of other imaginary landscapes
and the school with your name
teaches the liberty you exercised
in thought and by disposition
I know who you were in part
l'homme revolté from orthodox
devices of the man of letters

better you had been a Negro boxer
Shaw said what a thing to say
to a guest who had come so far

An in my study I shall view de wul'

Say it was then that I saw the shadows of men
in cane fields sharpen their machetes

in rhythm, pitch-perfect pitchfork labourers
who make the songs we hear on the radio

The sinews of their necks are active
as if scarred on a charcoal frieze, as if
eternity is their plot of arable ground

Their motion gives weight to things
otherwise of air, the dialect syllables

Although soon enough to be dead from overwork
and malnourishment, the black cane cutters

agree to keep time in the voice calling
while the tongue has breath behind it

and hands can wield and weld stanzas
from daylight: the craft of *here we dig*

Sheets of music at a white piano fluttering
bloom and the drift of a trumpet

The clatter of dishes, the car horns
the machinery of daylight breaking

open like two angel-wings of a bridge
the walkway to his dream is sundered

By all accounts these images are the
music that every heart would bless

precise, incalculable, transitory
like the trailing hair of orchid petals

on a girl you wanted a long time to kiss
and called *Joanie.*

KEI MILLER

A PRAYER FOR THE UNFLUMMOXED BEAVER

so unmoved by the boat's slow approach – the boat
drifting across the flat green acres of water; a prayer
for these acres of water which, in the soft light, seem firm;
the squirrels, however, are never fooled or taken in;
a prayer for the squirrels and their unknowable
but perfect paths – see how they run across
the twisting highway of cedars but never crash;
a prayer for the cedars and their dead knees rising
from the water like tombstones; a prayer for the cedar balls
that break when you touch them and stain
your fingers yellow, that release from their tiny bellies
the smell of old churches, of something holy;
a prayer for these alligators as holy as churches –
just last night when you thought of Hana
and her Cancer, you asked them to pray with you
knowing that their prayers are potent. At night
the grass is full of their red eyes; a prayer
for the grass that the alligators divide
in the shape of a never-ending S. You lean over
to pull it into the boat because your friend says
it can be cooked with salt and oil. She says in Burma
it is called Ka-Na-Paw; a prayer for the languages
that we know this landscape by; for the French as spoken
by fat fishermen, the fat fishermen who admit to the water –
we all dying. You understand? Savez?
A prayer for the dying that will come to all of us
but may it come soft as a boat drifting across the bayou;
may it find us unrattled and as unflummoxed as the beaver.

A WHO SEH SAMMY DEAD?

in three parts, for the escaped monkey

In July 2002, a monkey escaped from the Hope Zoo
     in Jamaica and was found dead, two days later,
     under a mango tree. Dogs had killed him.

1. Sammy plant piece-a corn down a gully

    ...tell them the corn wasn't really corn
but something you seeded, like maybe a dreadlock
from your rebel days in Honduras
hidden in soil so one day you'd remember
the fire
      the anger
              that some cities are worth burning –
  this was before
they reeled you in with fish net and had you
thrashing a let-mi-guh jungle dance,
khakiman clapping
     dancemonkeydance!
while you were bawling
     muuuuuurrrrrrrrtheerrrrrrr!
           or maybe the corn was your navel string –
call it what you will – it was planted
in a gully that wasn't a gully
  but is suh babylon call our homes
cause is not theirs
     Sammy, cümo se dice 'home'
             en español?

2. And it bear till it kill poor Sammy

    ...tell them the tree, once planted, will bear.
They thought you forgot Honduras,

thought you'd grown accustomed to the monotonous
grid of iron, to St. Thomas bananas and the flat
non-music of our dialect –
    they thought you were content making monkey
faces as trade for Snickers and lollipops,
      content passing collection hats
for blind organ grinders, content to scratch
your balls on camera.

    ...tell them Sammy, how you finally heard the tree
humming at night – how you've been jungle dreaming
and memories that died in your prison have risen
like Lazarus, zombie arms to choke you.
These past nights you woke crying
for mama
        crying for mambo and merengue and garifuna
          crying en español,

    Libertad! Libertad para mi!

3. *Sammy dead Sammy dead Sammy dead-o!*

...tell them your death is not really death
cause wasn't no shame in it – shame is
breath expired behind bars
    while your brothers find eternity
      in the jaws of cougars.

Your death is not death,
      only the separation of fur from spirit
    the ability to fly
      a monkey dream en español
homecoming, party, fiesta.

Your death is amen and amen,
      the swell-up of chains to bursting,

dugu, kumina, bienvenidos
    a Honduras otra vez!
A who seh Sammy dead? A who seh Sammy dead?
Tell them...
        tell them...
               Mi nuh dead-o!

DAVID MILLS

I mus' be about me Faddah's business
— Bob Marley

17 notes, lonely and moping, 17 lonely notes timid, tentative, 17 lonely notes pinched between Bob's fingers and his Gibson's acoustic strings. Wasn't with Jamaican nears and dears that I discovered Nesta. Was Wallingford, where rich kids smoked cloves, played hackey sack — soccer's impish, cousin — and ordered *za* with *shrooms*. That deleted *pi* sound a gust that could have tautened language's hammock — the lower lip — where that *mu* could have found refuge. But I guess two extra syllables would have weighed too much 'pon these kids tongue and teeth. After curfew, I would sneak down to Emile and Pete's room — a 16th note where I was the darkness that filled the dot. Sinsemilla smoke undulated like the ruffled hem of a calico dress. On those illicit evenings, my Park Avenue chums reacquainted me with myself while they reasoned 'bout roots Reggae. I listened to them — and Bob — on their tape deck. Sang along softly — a few words behind: "Ol Pirates, yes they, Rabbi..." *Rabbi? Gan — Jah Rastafari! Bob's not Jewish. It's Rob I, dude. Bob, Rob, they rhyme. Want a hit?"* Humiliated, I imagined pressing my fingers into sheet music, the staff — a five-stringed guitar, the bar lines, 19 frets. I would dig my fingers into that paper, that 19-measure neck, and like the room's smoke, sounds would rise from that sheet music, linger, stink. I wish ancestry were an audio cassette I could rewind six generations to the Scottish buccaneer who married a Jamaican woman. Back to where I could fully grasp that distant union's melody in my cells. After all, my father was the one born four years before Bob in the same St. Ann's Parish. And Nine Miles was not even nine miles from Brown's Town. So, why hadn't my mind rescued the West Indian side of my mouth? Why was I a sixteenth note incarcerated beyond this song's horizontal bars? Honestly, I felt besieged, closed in on by Bob's fretboard and the staff's five lines.

Emile's arrogance crushing me, but I could not lash out. Was I more Motown than Island; more Berry than Blackwell; more Marvin Gaye than Reg-gae – the accent always on the offbeat. I fished the J card of Marley's *Legend* from the cassette case. Bob's face reigned on the cover. Head tilted left, eyes skyward, right, forefinger curled under his bottom lip. As if, without that buoy of knuckles, he feared something might fall from the white side of his mouth. In Jamaica, there's a bay called Discovery where Uncle Sy let me splash in water as blue as his eyes. Now, huge and salty, now rippling and bombarded by swimsuits, one of his eyes became Puerto Seco's waters. After a dip, I walked on sand white and gritty as Uncle's hair. But in Wallingford, there was another bay of discovery that would have mocked a tale of sitting under the shade of a palm frond and feeling as if I were beneath the swollen shadow of Uncle's eyelashes. Would have cared less about the sixteen seasons after my last visit. How time had flown like those four notes before the last note before the first word of *Redemption Song*. But that 17th note, like those days during my 17th year, felt blunt and slow as some of music's bitter lessons.

THE FRONT COUNTRY

We loped down Standfast to the riot and whirr
of Brown's Town market. Between chipped
columns and beneath a corrugated roof, Dad,
like Uncle — who was paid to frisk produce —

fingered tamarinds and the sweet stink of mango.
Satisfied, Dad flagged down a van. Slid the side
door open: the sound like teeth biting a crisp June
plum. As I climbed in, my sandal slapped a puddle's

oily rainbow. I leaned my kinky noggin against a tinted
window: my thighs met by the prickle and balm of broken
upholstery and exposed padding. The driver — vexed
by shiftless GMC Rallys, Dodge Sportsmans, ankles

and insteps stalking soccer balls, and the occasional mangy
dog — yelled: a 50,000-year-old grouse. A sound one could trail
like Theseus' string back into the driver's maw, back through
labyrinths and passages to the first keen of human speech.

With the heel of his palm, he slammed the steering wheel
as if this were a karate class: the push and penetrate,
the technique and burst of adolescent pine board.
Beneath the tyres: coconut husks and shards of Red

Stripe crunched and popped. He sped off. Everyone
on board was pinched tight as a pack of menthol
Matterhorns. The V-8's hack and flatulence did not
keep him from playing chicken with other vans.

What of driving on a thoroughfare's left side?
A soft-voiced woman turned my way: "No worry,
I know G-d, and he's sitting next to me." Her thick,
lower lip, bordered: the sudden country chapped,

chocolate; the back country somewhere between
crimson and mauve. We passed mango trees, rockets
of corn. Had it been Saturday, Uncle would have carted
us the nine miles to Cousin Lindy's; would have whisked

us in his 1950s' white Zephyr: its pristine chassis always
made me feel like I was buckled in a cirrus cloud's plush
back seat. Made me forget the steering wheel was on
a car's passenger side. The van's window latch pulled up

and pushed out. A breeze: thick, warm as a bottle of Irish
Sea Moss orphaned on Granny's verandah. I held a gift
of Kelly's Strawberry Syrup in one hand, guzzled a bottle
of kola champagne with the other. A gravel-voiced DJ

yammered on the radio. No matter the mother, the tongue
is always pink speech; succinct meat; evidence of an icy's
escape plan; long-winded hanky; or song's stained carpet.
The WRJR jock spun *Land of my Birth* – a melody that seasoned

that August's air. I could not remember the verses, wondered why
words seemed to be so much about the mind, the mouth, but melodies
hummed and lurked in the chest's heaving grotto. I tagged along
with Donaldson's zesty, skipping rhythm, then sang the hook: "This

is the Land of my Birth. This is Jamaica, my Jamaica…"
That second syllable in Jamaica – that *ma* – made the front
of my tongue slope downward, so the lyrics might quicken
like a van hurtling toward Runaway Bay. The front tyre punched

a pothole, and my head nearly hit the roof of the Ford E-Series
while lyrics banged off the roof of my mouth. The honk
honking drove my forefingers to my ears. And as if an amp
had been lodged in my skull, my head resounded with song.

Oh, how I offered my twelve-year-old self to that chorus:
the delicious again and again of it. That summer of '78,
my mouth felt like a stadium of swaying Jamaicans, heads
held high: Donaldson's song an anthem. This, so soon

after that once unthinkable April where Nesta convinced
Manley and Edward to come together in a *feel all right*.
Sixteen years earlier, the October after the island's, Dad
had gained his independence and citizenship with winter.

Back then, I was not even a grunt in my father's underwear.
But on that August afternoon as the van shook like a drunk's
stomach, there were no *light throughs* nor *lest wes;* no songs
sounding as if a tongue had to snap to attention before words

– dry cleaned and spit shined – marched from a mouth. The tongue,
the palate: pink planets. Words: meteors born to burn beyond
these worlds, to escape spit's inner space and enter an atmosphere
incandescent with meaning, where syllable and sense gleam

and fizzle, slam and vanish, or fall silent, down like a wad
of bubble gum hawked from the driver's mouth. Gum stuck
to the van's floor mat; gum itching for the driver to open
his trap and bark in patois; gum that will gaze at the roof

of that driver's mouth – that blunt, pink planet – and though
dented by memory and teeth, gum that will sense that it is
the abandoned shadow of that celestial palate. That that hawking
could have only happened in August when the Perseids reach

their peak, when fragments are not just stone, but shards
of English broken and ancient; are sentences, fleeced of either
subject or verb, hurtling through space. A tattered green, gold
and black flag dangled from the van's rearview mirror. Yet,

there was no pomp, no circumstance, just a man — my father
— whose mouth often took twelve months to commit to a grin.
But on this afternoon in the second month that starts with *A*,
Dad's mouth was open, gap-toothed, brimming with glee

and song. One blood, one love: his mouth and mine, pass-
engers in a van whose driver believed traffic was a martial art.
Who had faith in how the heel of a palm inaugurates the blat
of a horn: who praised his steering wheel's *kiai* when it pummelled

Donaldson's tenor. Still, a few miles from *Runaway*, he ran
headlong into road, which dipped and curved like the side
of a tongue when it's been asked to keep the promise of song.

MONICA MINOTT

NO SALT

Grandy Nanny was no Bongo.
Bongo talk and talk all de time
but Grandy Nanny sight the play,
no singing on the ship on the way
over. No answer, no question
she dumb herself, swallow the
obeah, "till she reach land
then she shit it out". Grandy
Nanny fool dem, she eat no salt
so she could fly high, high above
the white blinding clouds. Bongo
never fly, only Maroon can fly.
So tomorrow morning
if you don't see me
me gone.

UPDATE ON THE NEW WORLD

The trees remembered
the pain of bringing forth
fruit, and called for Adam
to beat his ploughs into swords.
The sweat of generations before
turned to blood, and blood washed
the streets. Our brothers no longer faint
in fields at the hands of overseers.
They wake up wondering
who is to blame. Who is to blame?
Now that we are free, who is to blame?

PAMELA MORDECAI

LITANY ON THE LINE

Bad news again on the long distance line:
a growth flourishing in my sister's throat.
I think if one can spill hot coffee on oneself
and sue the restaurant and win, perhaps
a legal eagle with a well-tuned bill
could whistle up a case against AT&T
and Mama Bell. Two years ago on this
same phone, Lizzie told me and Mary Joan
that they'd shot Richard dead.
Across the trans-Atlantic line I hear
the ocean sizzle where infected earth
burning with fever oozes pus along a rupture in
its crust. I see the flickering photospores
inside the eyes of deep-sea fish. I hear

the cries of jettisoned black men,
women and children, not yet slaves, just worth
less than insurers paid for cargo spoiled en route.
Slitting this Carib basin's diamond skin
they flung its glints aside and burrowed in.
A person dies. It changes everything.
They died. No alteration? Nothing changed?
Except forever afterwards ships, boats
and planes with trained, skilled crews
and honed and hardened pilots fell
into that grave triangle for the Human Trade.
And flying now above the blue Bermudas, look
and you will see, along a coral ridge of white,
dark looping t's, like long canoes, like open crypts.
O, lay the ancestors to rest inside
these cursive curls with litanies.
Anoint their necks, their ankles, wrists,

with sacred oil. Put wampum shells upon
their eyes and set bouquets of trembling
anemones between their fingers and their toes.
Sing sankeys, beat the drums to dredge
up greed, harpoon it like Leviathan
and beach it where the carrion birds will pick
its pink meat from its bones. Blessed are you
buried in this blue dirt. Blessed are you
who never reached this side. Blessed are you
who listen as the tribe burbles its grievous news
across these fibre-optic threads. Blessed are you.

MERVYN MORRIS

CABAL

Dem beg him, beg him, till dem sick
an tired – him wouldn sign him name
to what de most a dem waan lick
de opposition with. Him seh, "Same

knife stick sheep stick goat," an walk
out of de room. De big-man bus
a funny laugh. Nobody never talk
to him like dat. Him seh, "Trust

me, eediot mus learn." So, first of all,
we kick de eediot out de group. An den
we start de rumour seh him bawl
fi mercy when we check de books again –

yuh never know him tief? Yes man, tief
like puss, unless yuh watchin him! An now
dat him get expose, pure grief
to get another job. Him shoulda bow!

Me scratch your back, you scratch mine;
but if yuh tun traitor yuh must pay.
Dyamn fool! De eediot bwoy was tryin
to block de road. We move him out de way.

A POET OF THE PEOPLE

The pressure of the public made it smart
to turn away from "self-indulgent Art".
He found immediate applause inviting,
and gave himself wholeheartedly to writing
poems for the people, loud and clear.

When people didn't seem to care
much whether he wrote well or not –
how was nothing, everything was what –
he changed his mind again. And so,
thinking to have another go
at "self-indulgent Art", he turned
towards the woman he had spurned,
his ever-loving personal Muse,
believing she could not refuse
him. But she did. She left him there,
writing for the people, loud and clear.

REPRISE

What now if honesty should choose
To say, in all this world's confusion,
That we are still too young for disillusion?

Well, that was 1962.

And here we are, a fractured nation
jumping up in celebration
of fifty years of chattering pretence
at independence,

though decades of political confusion
have made the growing rough,
and we're now old enough
for disillusion.

MUTABARUKA

LUCKY

PRISONER OR SLAVE
NOBODY CAN STOP REGGAE
REGGAE STRONG
SPIRIT OF HOPE
CAST IN GREED AND HATE
FATE ALONE CAN DECIDE… WHO SHALL LIVE
OR WHO WILL DIE
CAUGHT IN TIDES OF HATE
SINGIN SONGS OF JOY
REGGAE SONGS
SONGS OF JOY
SONGS OF RESISTANCE

AM I A SLAVE
PRISONER OR SLAVE
THE WORLD HEAR
THE CRY IS HEARD
FROM JAMAICA TO JO'BURG
I REMEMBER… I'M A PRISONER
WE ARE ALL PRISONERS… OF THE SYSTEM
OF POLITICIANS AND PREACHERS
OF LITTLE BOYS IN THE STREET WITH GUNS

SO WHO CAN SAY THEY'RE LUCKY
TO GO BEYOND WHAT IS THEIR FATE
WHO CAN GO BEYOND AND SING… SHOUT ALOUD
IN SONGS AND POEMS
ABOUT FREEDOM OF A PEOPLE
WANTING
HOPIN TO BE FREE
LUCKY ARE WE TO HAVE HAD LUCKY

THE BULLETS ECHO
BUT
THE BALLADS ECHO
REACHIN FURTHER THAN ANY BULLETS CAN
PIERCIN THE HEARTS OF MANY WHO SEEK FREEDOM
WE ARE LUCKY
NOBODY CAN STOP REGGAE
REGGAE STRONG

SPIRIT OF HOPE
SO WE ARE LUCKY
BULLETS CANNOT… WILL NOT STOP REGGAE
LUCKY ARE WE
TO FALL THEN RISE
LIFTIN UP THE WORLD
SHOUTIN CHANTIN SINGIN SONGS OF FREEDOM

FOR THOSE YET TO BORN
IN THIS WORLD OF BULLETS
AND LITTLE BOYS ON STREETS
FILLED WITH HATE AND GRIEF
STREETS OF GOLD AND LEAD
BLOOD RED
THICK BLOOD LIKE MORNING MIST
IT STOPS US FROM SEEIN
WHAT LIES AHEAD

BUT THIS MUSIC
THIS… REGGAE MUSIC
BRINGS A WIND
THAT BLOWS AWAY THIS MISTY MORNIN
MOVIN THE SHACKLES FROM THESE
PRISONERS
THESE SLAVES
WAITIN ON THE RIGHT TIME
WHEN THESE LITTLE BOYS WITH BULLETS OF HATE

WILL LISTEN TO THE SOUND OF HOPE
AND BECOME LUCKY
AND NOMORE
WILL THEY BE PRISONERS OF SLAVES

SO THE CHANT IS OUT
LUCKY ARE WE
NOBODY CAN STOP REGGAE
REGGAE STRONG

GEOFFREY PHILP

A PRAYER FOR MY CHILDREN

When you find yourself in a faraway land
surrounded by men, animals that mutter strange
sounds, do not be afraid: neither you, your parents,

nor your ancestors have ever been alone.
So trust the earth to bear you up, follow
the wind as it leads you through valleys

clustered with trees heavy with fruit –
some that seem familiar enough to eat,
but you still aren't sure they are the same

as the ones you left on the other side
of the river that you've now forgotten.
Eat. Feast on the bounty. Feed the fire

that burns away the knot in your stomach,
sets ablaze the horizon, all that your eyes
can see – that has been promised to you

since your cry pierced the morning air:
your parents bathed you with kisses,
baptized you with caresses,

swaddled you in care before you uttered
your first words to the moon, sun, stars,
wobbled your first steps into unknowing –

all the while rising into your inheritance.
And if you awaken under the branches of a cotton tree,
cradled in its roots, draw a circle around yourself

and all those whom you love, cross
yourself three times before you step
over the threshold. Welcome the ancestors,

all the kindly spirits who have followed you,
your parents across many seas, oceans,
and deserts; entertain them with strong drink

and soft food: rice, yams, bananas, the ever-
present rum to bless the hands that have lifted
you up, and sanctified the place you now call home.

JANETT PLUMMER

THE HOUSE

The house was beautiful, it was
big, wide and wondrous,
grand ceilings festooned with ornate roses,
diaphanous curtains billowing gracefully around tall windows.

And the husband who never married me
did not come to fix the pipe that leaked water over the patio,
while it gushed harder than the wet drops cascading my cheeks,
until a man, borrowed from a friend, and his spanner, screwed
the waterworks shut 'til floor and cheek were dry.

The grand roof let out heat by the kilowatt when poinsettias littered
        the garden,
forced warmth into humid August nights.
The doors kept out all manner of infidels,
the windows let light shimmy in faithfully.

The babies I strained to carry, which never arrived,
did not swing on the triple swing;
two seats remain as new.

I shopped in antique stores alone,
paying for oak tables with banknotes redder than my fury.
The curtains still waft, graceful, lonesome.
One winter, I left the house, alone.

VELMA POLLARD

ROADS
(Remembering Aimé Césaire)

"your roads are good"
I heard me tell the great man
asking how a stranger felt
"but yours are yours" he said

inside this chain of islands
roads tell silently
or shout who owns
who does not own

so answering my young guest
veering flustered
from roads surprising good
to roads surprising bad

"I wish your roads were either
always good or always bad"
"these roads are ours" I say
"just like the bamboo beauty
marvel that you see"

This is my land
my country courting death to mangroves
death to breeding fish
to coral and to trees
wasting our permanence for homes to
transient guests who may or may not come

This is my land
Jamaica to the world
high speed

high art
high music and high thought
currents surprising strong

and peerless mountain beauty
leaping my heart anew
tears in glad eyes

the world looks on
with open mouth
these roads are ours

CLAUDIA RANKINE

MARY JANE SEACOLE REMIX

In a starched, white performance,
she begins to unpack her medicine bag
from which flies the Doctor Bird
whose shadow stains her face
like a map I recognize by shape from a distance
even as she is there in front of me, a relation
with all the resemblance of a nation.
I have to tell her ours is the new way to live,
our bodies, weighted with its high, high pressure,
expanding to carry the time between us.

She is in a hurry, on her way to the anniversary
of the independence she insists is from slavery
by another name. We are in this other
country, in my century, despite being born
on the same soil in that place of wood and water,
a place older than my years by only a year
though it was always there in the way
existence floats above colonies as the land
absorbs settlers and queens. Why are you here
and not at home, she wants to know?

Her fingers linger on my forehead, distressed
there is bleeding as far as she can see.
I grow stronger with her scent,
deep, deep sea, and to answer her I must
triangulate this body with two countries
into the history painting still forming.
My tongue hollows out into the hull of a ship
and this she understands, this she realises
is alive in memory. That's when she covers
her mouth with mine and breathes in
the changing same because her sovereignty,
all her life, was unsettling this body from the start.

128

HEATHER ROYES

MARGUERITA THE RHUMBA QUEEN FROM CLUB HAVANA

Uptown and downtown boys trembled in their sleep
waking in wet and sweaty sheets —
dreaming of Marguerita the Rhumba Queen from Club Havana.
No mother, wife, or girlfriend knew
they had gone to see her dance,
to see her wine and shake her body.

But there was only one strong Don
who could blow her horn, one Don,
one rebel daughter of a Lebanese fishmonger:
two troubled souls.
Dungu Malungu, she called it.

On New Year's Day, 1965,
she came home at 3.16 in the morning
wet and tired from the club;
threw herself on the bed, but he,
furious for having overslept,
and konked out on herbs and jealousy,
was waiting for her.

At 3.17 on New Year's day, 1965,
he fell on her with his knife
plunging into her chest.
"OH, JunieJunieJunie, NO!"
And the second time, he lunged
full strength into her chest again.

The third time, he lay gently on her, panting,
paused and could not get up.
But he did, and then the fourth —

with all his force, he crashed into her body
until the knife blade broke off.
And she was still.

At 3.30, on New Year's Day in the morning, 1965,
The Don fell off the bed and,
lying on the floor, gazed with glazed eyes
at the ceiling, his hands
outstretched, covered with blood.

SAFFRON

UNEVEN-ING

it was always the evening
that bothered me

the starchy jagged mornings
hide no hypocrites
when the honest sun pierces
the undecided sleepiness below
the Blue Mountains

the gaping yawn of morning
holds promises that may stretch
into reality as it ripens

midday is the brash mirror
tactlessly showing truths and lines
by our eyes – even while we squint
to narrow the brunt of the hit

night is the frank liberal
and what happens here should
remain hushed in its tombed heart –
the luxury of a vaulted secret
as plush as the pile of its cover

but evenings and leavenings
and ambiguous lighting, shadows
changing views and swirling
insecurities – tensions squirm
some release without the true
abandon of night
this is the time
for thieves and liars, edges of daggers
sharp, but evening

OLIVE SENIOR

THE WHY OF EVERYTHING
"Death's needle looking for thread…"
— Pablo Neruda, *"Solo la muerte"*

Death in our yard is a three-foot horse, a hearse
      is a discord, a terse way of life
      is a blanket of dread
      is a bloodstain that's spreading and spreading

Death is a bullet with one name on it
But death cannot read
and death cannot count
and death comes rattling in with bullets for all
and death is five dead and
one blue note
death is the fire in the hut
the machete in the night
the toddler playing in the dirt
      on the pathway of revenge

Death rankles as the wound in the soul of the one
who was a no-name child just like this one
who left school without an A or an X
no certificate of belonging, of knowing who he is
or what he came on earth for

Death says:
I would kill to know who I am
My gun is my family
I carve my own bloodlines
I emblazon my names in the headlines

Death is the needle looking for thread

Death is the engine that runs out of fuel
The early blooming flower that falls too soon
the light bulb that blows in the moment that's critical

Death is the pain without end, the crucible
the chalk-marks on the floor
the galliwasps's gaze
the x of the cross
the cracks in the glaze
the hunt for a cure that runs out of steam
the closing of the door
the scorpion's sting
the malicious intent
the act of revenge
the lighthouse lamp that fails

Death is the out of in, the upside down
the zag of zig, the turnaround

Death is the marrow in the meat
the matter in the spirit
the rumble in the street

Death is the not going gently
death is aim and trajectory, the bullet
from a grassy knoll

Death is the uprising, the indwelling
the unforgiving

Death is the calculator with no symbol
but subtraction and the x of extinguish
excision exclusion expiry expulsion
extirpate extraction extradition exit

Death stalks without fear or favour
death enters each life equally
death is the true democracy
better than the ballot at choosing randomly
or targeting if that's your preference
Death is the ultimate job-seeker needing no reference

Death is the needle looking for thread

Once death sat inside an enclosure
a monument to pride and achievement
a listing on marble of names and their good deeds
But death knows death knows death knows
where the thread goes
                    Death could not sit long with
hypocrisy; walked over that fence and out of
that cemetery, shunned the hollow promise of
consecrated ground, walked into the town to seek
justice. To gather names to engrave on that house
                    For a cemetery is only a dormitory
They say that duppy blessed with holy water
is the baddest duppy. And the ones that are bred
in the tombs of hypocrisy have dog-heart
No conscience
Yet all will fall to the reaper

Death is the needle looking for thread

In the cemetery the dead are laid out like the living
the poverty-stricken, the nameless, still have their slums
the churchical lie together waiting for the revelator
the BIG MAN lies in his house of death with wife
and children: a bloodline. Shanties and mansions together
rest. The needle makes connections manifest

Holes in the ground are houses too
for the victims that are nameless
but their eyes have registered you
Who knows, who knows where the needle goes
looking for thread to sew up the lips of those
who give tips: the dead informers

Death is the needle looking for thread

Death is lamentation, Ezekiel
and chariots of fire. Death is revelation
and horsemen travelling two by two or
in packs or in posses. In cars and planes and
trains, on foot, on camel, on asses. Death shall not
let them lightly pass. It snares or pricks whom
it chooses

Death is the needle looking for thread

The thread that's a red, red line through history
that loops and curls and knots like a net
of discovery, entrapping pirates, bankers and
cutlass blades, planters' whips and sinews
of slaves, politicians' lying tongues and the
rachet knife cutting the root of innocence
the bullet's trajectory riding on collusion:
richman poorman beggarman thief
policeman businessman presidents and those
that preach. If any pass through thread's weave
as knots work loose, the thread will be dragged
by the needle of truth

With wide open eye, the needle passes
through doors, through secrets, through lies
some might fall through thread's weave, some are
caught in the knots, thread makes no judgement
it is the needle that plots.

So, MAKE WAY! MAKE WAY!
Looking for thread, looking for thread
to bind up the wounds of the lost, the betrayed
from the towers of commerce to the door of the church
to the shanties of the poor where the johncrows perch
no parliament here only tenements of fear

Sinnerman, there is no way out, no consulate
Here one finds neither passport nor visa
only this vine here that looks like a sign there
like a thread to the exit of the maze of your life
and the bloodied signs you left on the way
your fingerprints netted as clear as day
as you pass through the eye of scrutiny

If justice on earth has too wide a weave
the snare of the cemetery is tight like a sieve
like a noose, like the knot of judgement.

The needle will always find the thread.

TANYA SHIRLEY

FLOWER GIRL

Her mother placed two red cushions
on a dining room chair lifted her high
into the air then settled her atop with
a firm hand and a kiss on the forehead.

The hot comb began its virgin trek
through tangled coils; the brown child
knitted her brows and before the comb
could straighten a new tuft of tight curls

she released a howl, the kind that scares
the prey and shatters ribs on its way
out the body, the body skilled in contortion,
pushing the limit of limbs and restraints.

You can't be a flower girl with nappy hair.
You want to spoil your aunty's wedding?
Is shame you want to shame we?

How much more shame could this child cause?
Wasn't it enough that now we knew
she was part animal, capable of breaking
atoms and dreams with her screams?

The hairdresser cooed and cajoled
but she was no match for this child
who had not yet learned that vanity
will make women walk through fire.

The child threw herself to the ground
yanked off her yellow dress, heaved
and heaved, rolled and spun her eyes
into half moons, the room growing red.

Give the pickney two good lick!
Is them kind of pickney turn round box
them own mother and father.

But the poor mother was transfixed.
Each convulsion a rip in the umbilical cord.
Where did a child like this come from and how
do you mother this?

The child spewed venomous vomit
on to the rug then gasped for holy air.
The army of aunts swooped down, carried her
into the tub, turned on the cold water full-force.

We rebuke you Satan! Jesus! Jesus!
We cast you out Satan! Jesus! Jesus!
Devil come out! Jesus! Jesus!

The child gripped the side of the tub, looked up
to the heavens hidden behind the ceiling
then fell asleep, the aunts wondering,
What do we do with her hair?

A-DZIKO SIMBA

PIECE IN PARTS (FI TOSH – R.I.P.)

Tales from the Pen 10

One – Dem

The massive are at the gateway.
They will always be
clamouring crowds
merged meat of mawga meagre means
desires pressed down, piled up, push back
'gainst iron
fists' tight hold
of the too little for the too many massives.
Mean.
While
inside
the compound of *these* people
sitting pretty, damning
those people
fingers pointed
one out
three back
too black
those people
these black-too kiaan tek
these black-too people damning
those black-too they
black-too just
kiaan tek.

Two — Daak Dem Daak

In the dark of the bun-bun
stuffed in, packed down
to the barrel bottom
wet and renk
black and brown.
roaches breed.

Three — Di Part Dem

Say a prayer for
the soon to be
deportees.
A prayer prior to being
unemployed.
Prayer prior to being
drunk and disorderly.
Prayer prior to being
down and out a
prayer prior to being
in the streets, on the streets, of the streets,
to being the streets themselves.
Say a prayer prior to being
Not.
A prayer prior to not being, being a not being being.
Being past,
being tense,
being zero,
being none.
A prayer prior to non-being.

Four — Waan Dem

Scan dem.
Can dem.
Pen dem.
Condemn dem
not-us-alien-immigrant-ghetto-dweller-others-not-us.
Not us.
Not-me-not-you *dem*.
The cursed curs.
Pariah dogs prowling
sacred suburbs
with audacity.
Packs packing.
Send dem packing.
Scan dem.
Can dem.
Pen dem.
Condemn dem
not-us-alien-immigrant-ghetto-dweller-others-not-us.
Not us.

Five — Prii Dem

What you pray
flimsy as
what you build
collapses under the clamouring crowd.

What fortress can withstand
the moral might?
The massive swarm
on rock. on stone. on sand.

Breach the boundaries.
No quick solution.
No be gone Baygon to spray.

What you pray
flimsy as
what you build
collapses under the clamouring crowd.
Rock, stone, sand
shifts
in time.
With time,
sand shifts.

Six – Dam Dem

Say a prayer.
Say a prayer to the god of
bombo bloodclaat.
Say a prayer.

No one but the massive
know where the barrels be buried.

Not even the numbers
can count themselves.

Say a prayer
to curse the cursed
and abused.

Say a pray
for your blood brothers
who even water you refuse.

Say a pray
for your soul
and say it fast
and say it like you mean it.
Say it a million times a million times a million.
Mantra it.
Say all the prayers you want
to Bombo Bloodclaat.

Seven – Di Rieza Dem a Step

They don't want no piece.
All they want is
equal rights
and justice.

MARY LOU SOUTAR-HYNES

INDEPENDENCE:
EARLY YEARS

What is it about islands and anthems –
adrenal imperatives,   passions coiled in back and limbs,   roots at home,
       routes away,

how long a note is held –
                                        edginess of shores
                         unfixed,   linger and release,
                                fascia tightening

The summer we renewed our vows –
Kingston dancehall-nights and moonlight thrusting through
the convent's louvred windows –
         poverty, chastity, obedience, vows of service –
              August's belching heat

                    where the land is green

No journey too far through Manchester hills for three young nuns
and their white Cortina station wagon,   fresh as Mandeville rain,
and as persistent –
                 soliciting for the high school fundraiser –
a farmer to donate the suckling for slaughter,   the meat packer's freezer
where it hung for a week,   a baker's midnight oven,
and the finished deed on spinning spits that sparkling crowd-filled
       afternoon

                    and the sun shines

Not much older than her Fifth Form students,   she mounts their poetry
        on classroom walls and at the public library –
no imperative to mimic or dissemble   on topics they know least

                              better to reach   for the syntax of freedom,
           home-turf semantics,   felt sense,
                      tugging at the sea

               '   A search   for grammars of authority,
           words and deeds that seek and find their truth,
                      mindscapes for imagining   and fine lines between —

           those surprising moments,   shadings and imperfections,   when
                      the sun comes out   bending notes —

                      curves and gestures   shoreline's limen
                         'the island's edge of everything

ANDREW STONE

THE GARDENER

The yellow sun beats down
on this dark earth, and grass,
once wild, is now a manicured lawn,
neat, like the cornrows of the gardener's hair.
Daytime is the flat surface of an iron
pressing moisture out. The retreating damp
carries an exotic mix: last night's rain,
morning sweat, fragrant flowers, stale piss,
and blood. No welts on this labourer's back;
slavery is dead and memory buried along with it!
He wears a keloid scar like a trophy
of more modern conflicts. No mission,
no passion beyond the boundary lines
of this property. Unwilling to read, to look,
he misses the sign, remains ignorant
of the title stencilled on his heart.

FABIAN THOMAS

L'ACADCO
(for Dr. L'Antoinette Osunide Stines)

we are
pocomania and pointe shoes
classical ballet and kumina
wi can
butterfly and willie bounce
do di tattie, worl dance, dutty wine but also
fouette and gran battement
execute L'Antech, Horton, Graham

we are
the Middle Passage,
the African Diaspora
British-ruled.
Independent.
Brukins
Jonkanoo
Kum inna dis!

we are Jamaican
                Ashanti
Cromanti,
        Taino
Carib
Oshun
Shango
Downtown
Uptown

We are L'ACADCO
A United Caribbean Dance Force!

Did the dolphins know
merrily swimming astern
the hell in the hold?

RALPH THOMPSON

SEASONS

After a hard winter
Spring wafts in the window
smelling of thawed soil and cut grass.
Thus langueur begins,
(I am studying French in a strange land
quartered by seasons),
mope and nope caught up in my reveries
stalling the affairs of men.

I imagine a young girl skipping rope,
levitating at the apogee of jump,
floating off into a Chagall painting:
a conquistador parks his pike in a corner,
mumbling mañana, and Vivaldi,
after a night's adventure, knows the score
but will not lift a fist to note
a minim or a quaver… later… later.

I look through the open window
and even in the torpor of this interregnum,
I can see in my village
bougainvillea bursting into bloom,
the frank tumescence of anthurium lilies,
the whole seething, teeming, heaving,
jig, jiggle, jerk and jolt of year round germination,
a pregnant girl sashaying confidently by,
a summer in her step, a belly full of hope.
The French language, I have learned,
has no single word for what I mean by homesickness.
J'ai le mal du pays!
Lord, how I miss my island.

DONNA AZA WEIR-SOLEY

TERESA MATILDA MCCALLA MCCALLA

To feel the weight of a loss that ungrounds you
and yet not know its source is a cruelty
only human memory could design.

For years I felt adrift from my moorings,
anchorless in uncharted waters
never really understanding why
until I took a train from Oxford to Sheffield
to find you waiting on a mantelpiece
in Uncle Brisente's living room,
your oval face nicely framed in silver,
skin tinged a reddish-bronze glow,
warm and fragrant like pimento.
In your floral skirt and crisp round-collar white blouse,
your long bony hands crossed in your lap,
you could have been dressed for Wednesday-night prayer meeting.
Grandma, your eyes held the high purple of the St. Catherine hills,
and the promise of rain water.

I brought your picture back to New York with me
to copy and distribute to the family
who were losing you, Mummah, bit by precious bit.

The first night back you dreamt me
red over-ripe coffee beans
I woke up smelling their sickly-sweet aroma
feeling the damp earth of the coffee walk
and hearing the chick-man-chicks singing in the pear tree.

You said you were tired
had been picking pimento in Fustick Hill
and gathering coffee from Breeze Mill,

asked me to pick the red, pity-me-lickle ants from your skin,
rub your feet with bay rum.

You were harvesting your crops to save
for Bertina's plane ticket to America,
Brisente's passage to England,
and no, you couldn't stop to rest or talk with me
because, didn't I see, there was so much work to be done,
the gungo peas not yet on the fire for dinner,
and what would Mass Knoll say
when him come back from the fields
and no dinner nuh ready?

So I walked with you to the dirt-floor kitchen
and swept the fire-hearth while you gathered firewood.
I watched your eyes redden from the smoke
as you blew into the brushwood to get the fire started
and sat back, coughing, as tiny flames leapt up
devouring the brushwood and igniting the logs
under your three-legged dutch pot.

When your pot was bubbling with green gungo peas,
salt beef, white flour dumplings and soft white yam,
you filled your clay pipe with plug tobacco
and lit it. Turning the bowl inside your mouth,
you rocked back on your heels on the hard-packed dirt,
your long floral skirt fanning out round you,
rings of smoke forming 'round your head
and said:

Lissen good --

Ah was born Teresa Matilda Toban,
but evvy badda call mi Miss Mattie or Sistah Mattie.
Mi madda was an African 'oman, Maroon, fighter people dem
she was a healer an a midwife.

151

Mi daddy people dem come from India
im come 'ere wen im a bway
an start cut sugar cane from im inna short pants.
Mi daddy had a wandring spirit.
Couldn't sit one place fe long.
Mi Madda, she know all a de ole African ways.
Some she teach me, some me feget;
but de herbs business, dat one stick wid me.

Mi nevah have a easy life —
mi born inna struggle
mi birth fourteen pickney.
One born dead,
one get poliomylitis from im a baby,
one get a bad injection almost cripple im.

Mi bury two husband —
cousin dem, same name:
one jet black and cool like de stone in im water jar,
de odder one red like wite people,
eye dem green like de pickney dem glass marble.
Dem did love me, de two a dem, inna fe dem way,
but de fus one cubbitch and prideful,
im never could forgive im people dem,
who tun dem back wen im married me.
Never did forgive me fe being de reason.
De todder one cross, and got a wandrin spirit,
like mi daddy. Couldn't settle down,
walk out all de lan im buy and
de res dat im come find me wid,
never fine de peace im a walk a look fah.

Sun never ketch me inna bed
so me no know wha sunlight
feel like thru de window inna yuh face,
but me know bout donkey pad-up wid clothes

fe go a river before day bruk Monday morning
an me know bout holding de head
of somebody you love in you lap
till de last breath leave dem body
and watching you pickney dem catch plane and ship,
one by one, two by two, gawn a foreign,
an you don't know if you gwine live to see dem
come back home again.

Dese same hands help birth plenty grands into dis world,
plait plenty hair, and ease a dying woman from de heaviness
of stillbirth when de doctors give she over fe dead –
de same oman who never talk to me again
after she find out she couldn't mek no more baby.
Yes, me know bout hatred 'oman can have fi 'oman
fe nuh reason at all, an mi know say bad mine
sometimes worse dan obeah, an dat people can cubbitch yuh,
fe nuttin at all; all fe yuh children dem,
even when yuh an dem a suffah, an a suck salt grain.

Dese same hands know how fe boil up castor oil fe speed up lazy baby.
wash you in cerasee bath when you have chicken box,
boil yuh tamarind tea when yuh have measles,
wrap yuh up, so yuh sweat out good when you a roast wid dengue fever.

Dese hands is healing hands, hugging hands, and beating hands
to cut yuh lickle tail when yuh behave bad,
rub dixie peach and castor oil into your scalp
till yuh fall asleep, and a put yuh down beside me gentle.
Dese hands even teach yuh to pick rat-cut coffee beans, remember?

I woke up to a flood of memories long forgotten,
my pillow soaked in tears
the mumps that I got the same day you died,
and the long black hearse carrying your body past the gate
as I stood in what was left of the coffee walk –

the little bit the government had not killed with spraying:
killing ganja, they said; killing off de small coffee farmers, you said –
leaves, tied to my jaw to keep the swelling down,
held in place by a red kerchief,
the dull ache of the mumps competing with a tightness in my chest
my breathing shallow and laboured
your loss weighting down my eight year old spirit,
as if I had been orphaned.

Mummah, I carried your picture home from England
I know your spirit came with me
cause I dream your plug tobacco,
smell the camphor, the pimento and the bay rum in your skin,
see you in the grandmothers waiting at the bus stop,
sitting in the pew across from me at Church.

And often, when I forget the source of my own power,
it is your voice that soothes me still,
your hands rubbing bay-rum into my neck,
that gets me through these nightmare days,
my dreams trailing red-ripe coffee beans,
leading from you and back to myself.

D'BI.YOUNG

REVOLUSHUN

mi waan fi ask fiwi people if wi have amnesia
inna jamaica nuff a wi a fallah
di u s of imperialist amerikkka
wid wi benz, we lex, and of course wi beama

fame, money and drugs is whe we a defend
nobody nuh remembah way back when
di maroons did fight against wi enslavement
kill off did yam english, spanish and french

send dem back whe dem cum from, gain wi independence
united we stand, di divided mus repent

where di british leave off, di amerikkkans start
dem want a new playground when cuba kick dem raas
going all around di world selling amerikkkan dreams
jamaicans don't buy dis imperialist scheme

dem tief di resources and di land, dem suh bold
export crack-cocaine fi kill di young and di old
biggest arms smugglers pon disya world scene
dem give wi youths big guns to kill their bright ghetto dreams

polticians don't give raas about di state of di country
dem sellout to amerikkka fi mek nuff money
bogus elecshun wid only two party
have jamaicans kill jamaicans while dem feel irie

if yuh walk pon ghetto street whole heap a starving pickney
govament nah provide no opportunity
people mus have access to basic necessity

only a revolushun will end disya poverty
only a revolushun will find a solushun
only a revolution will save fiwi nation

NOTES

p. 86-95: "Farewell to Clarendon"
Claude McKay's verses, printed in italics above, appear in *Complete Poems* (2004), edited by William J. Maxwell. Drawn from this text, the lines for "50 verses for 50 years" were chosen by a fixed procedure: each line is the fifth from the top of every fifth page of the poems. The lines were written down according to the editor's sequence and then paired into couplets. Some couplets invert the position of the two lines in the pair, but all together they advance from the earliest dialect poems of 1911-1912 to the poems written near the end of his life, in the 1940s. (The phrase "here we dig" is traditional.)

p. 137: "Independence: Early Years"
The lines: *where the land is green; and the sun shines* are variations on the explanation of two of the three colours of the Jamaican flag: green and gold, respectively. Poverty, chastity, obedience and the service of the poor, sick and ignorant were vows taken by members of the Order of Religious Sisters of Mercy. Found images "roots at home/ routes away," and "edginess" are from "Littoral Space(s): Liquid Edges of Poetic Possibility," Suzanne Thomas, *Journal of the Canadian Association for Curriculum Studies*, Vol. 5, No. 1, Spring/Summer 2007.

p. 140: "L'ACADCO"
A United Caribbean Dance Force is one of Jamaica's renowned dance companies. Founder and Artistic Director, L'Antoinette Stines moved back to her homeland Jamaica in 1982 and has since then spearheaded the revolutionary fusion of rich Caribbean folklore with contemporary themes in an original and distinctive language/ technique called L'Antech. Ms. Stines and L'ACADCO have become dynamic ambassadors for Jamaican and Caribbean cultures and advocates for its sustained development and preservation.

ABOUT THE CONTRIBUTORS

Opal Palmer Adisa was born in Jamaica and received her PhD from The University of California, Berkeley. A recipient of a Bi-national Fulbright Commission Residency, a Cave Canem Fellowship, and the PEN Oakland/Josephine Mills Award, she is the editor of *The Caribbean Writer*. She has published several books of prose and poetry, including the poetry collections *Eros Muse*, *Caribbean Passion*, and *Tamarind and Mango Woman* and short story collections *Until Judgment Comes* and *Bake-Face and Other Guava Stories* as well as the novels *It Begins With Tears* and *Painting Away Regrets*. A professor of Creative Writing, Literature, and Diversity Studies at California College of the Arts, she co-edited the 2011 anthology *Caribbean Erotic: Poetry, Prose & Essays* with Donna Weir-Soley, published by Peepal Tree Press.

Lillian Allen hails from Spanish Town, Jamaica and lives in Toronto, Canada where she is a Professor of Creative Writing at the Ontario College of Art & Design University. Internationally renowned as a leading dub poet, writer and multidimensional artist, she has garnered two Juno awards for recordings of her dub poetry with music for *Revolutionary Tea Party* and *Conditions Critical*. Other discs include *Nothing But A Hero* and *Freedom and Dance*. She has published six books of poetry including *Psychic Unrest*, *Women Do This Everyday*, *Why Me*, *If You See Truth*, *The Teeth of the Whirlwind* and *Rhythm an' Hardtimes*.

Edward Baugh is Professor Emeritus of English, University of the West Indies, Mona. He was born in the town of Port Antonio, Jamaica, and educated at the University College of the West Indies, Queens University in Ontario, Canada, and the University of Manchester. His book *Derek Walcott, a critical study*, was published in 2006; his most recent book is *Frank Collymore: A Biography*. His two published poetry collections are *A Tale from the Rainforest* and *It Was the Singing*. Two compact discs of his readings have also appeared: *Edward Baugh: Poems from "It Was the Singing"* and *Edward Baugh Reading from His Poems*.

Jacqueline Bishop was born and grew up in Kingston, but as a child spent her summer holidays in the small district of Nonsuch, deep in the mountains of Portland. She left to join her mother in the USA where she completed her education. She is a poet, novelist, artist and filmmaker and critic. She has published two collections of poetry, *Fauna* and *Snapshots from Istanbul*, a novel, *The River's Song* and edited *Writers who Paint, Painters Who Write*, about the work of Jamaican artist/poets – all published by Peepal Tree Press. She is also the author of *My Mother Who Is Me: Lifestories from Jamaican Women in New York*. She was the founding editor of *Calabash: A Journal of Caribbean Arts & Letters*. She lives and works in New York City.

Jean "Binta" Breeze, an actress and poet, grew up in rural Jamaica before moving to Kingston, where she soon established herself as a writer, performer, and recording artist. Often backed by the rhythms of reggae, Breeze became well known as a dub poet in London, and recorded the album *Tracks* with the Dennis Bovell Dub Band. She studied at what was then the Jamaica School of Drama, now the Edna Manley College of the Visual and Performing Arts. Her publications include *Ryddim Ravings and Other Poems*, which was also released as an album, *Spring Cleaning*, *On the Edge of an Island*, *Song Lines*, *The Arrival of Brighteye and Other Poems* and *The Fifth Figure*. Her most recent book of poems, *Third World Girl: Selected Poems*, was published in 2011.

Lloyd W. Brown was born in Jamaica. He graduated from the University of the West Indies and emigrated to Canada where he did graduate work and taught before moving to the United States. He was Professor of Comparative Literature at the University of Southern California for many years before his retirement. He has written a book on Jane Austen's fiction, edited a collection of essays, *The Black Writer in Africa and the Americas* (1973) and the pioneering *West Indian Poetry* (1978, 1984), the first such survey in this field, which focuses on the work of McKay, Walcott and Brathwaite. He has written numerous articles for European, North American and Caribbean journals. His poetry was first published in the collection, *Duppies* (Peepal Tree).

Frances Coke was born in Jamaica. An educator, she has been writing since her early twenties. She has written fiction and drama for stage and radio. Her first volume of poems, *The Balm of Dusk Lilies*, was published in 2001 by The Jamaica Observer Literary Publications and her second volume, *Intersections,* was published by Peepal Tree Press in 2010. Her poems have been published in The Jamaica Observer Literary series, *Bearing Witness 1, 2, and 3; Kunapipi (Journal of Postcolonial Writing)*, and *The Caribbean Writer*. She was awarded The Daily News Prize for Poetry by *The Caribbean Writer* in 2008.

Mel Cooke was born on November 21, 1971. That decade's political turmoil and the 1980s' explosion of dancehall music continue to have an impact on his writing. A writer with *The Gleaner* since 2000, he applies a journalistic approach to recording events as poetry. A Calabash workshop participant, Cooke is the author of a book of poems titled *11/9* (2008).

Christine Craig was born in Kingston, but spent much of her early years in rural St. Elizabeth. She is a graduate of the University of the West Indies and has published short stories, poems and children's fiction. Her latest collection of poems, *All Things Bright*, includes a reprint of her first collection *Quadrille for Tigers*. It was published by Peepal Tree Press, in 2010.

Kwame Dawes was born in Ghana in 1962, the son of the Jamaican poet and novelist, Neville Dawes. He grew up in Jamaica, did his first degree at UWI, Mona and completed his postgraduate education in Canada. He has published seventeen collections of poetry, two poetry anthologies, three works of fiction, four works of nonfiction and a play. His most recent poetry collection is *Wheels*, published by Peepal Tree in 2012. Formerly based at the University of South Carolina, he is currently the Glenna Luschei Editor of *Prairie Schooner* at the University of Nebraska, where he is a Chancellor's Professor of English. He is a faculty member of Cave Canem, and associate poetry editor at Peepal Tree Press. In 2009 he won an Emmy Award for his work on www.LiveHopeLove.com, a mulltimedia website on the human face of HIV/AIDS in Jamaica, a project that inspired the collection *Hope's Hospice*.

Richard "Dingo" Dingwall started writing in 1994 and joined the Jamaica Poetry Society in 1995. He recorded the album *Ransom* in 2000, a blend of music and poetry; a video for the song "Earth Speaks" was voted Video of the Year by the Caribbean Broadcasting Union. A winner of the Caribbean Music Expo talent search in 2001, Dingo has been featured at the Calabash Literary Festival, Reggae Sumfest with the Zinc Fence Band, and at Reggae Sunsplash 2006. He is currently working on material for a second album.

Marcia Douglas was born in the UK of Jamaican parents in 1961, but grew up in rural Jamaica. She left Jamaica in 1990 to study for a Master of Fine Arts in Creative Writing at Ohio State University and was awarded a Ph D in African American and Caribbean Literature in 1997. Her first collection of poems, *Electricity Comes to Cocoa Bottom* (Peepal Tree) won a Poetry Book Society recommendation. She has published two novels, *Madam Fate* and *Notes from a Writer's Book of Cures and Spells* (Peepal Tree). She teaches at the University of Colorado, Boulder.

Makesha Evans was the recipient of a fellowship with the Calabash International Literary Festival Trust. She was published in the anthology *So Much Things to Say* and was a co-facilitator of the *Manifesto Jamaica* poetry workshop in 2010. Evans is a psychologist and a Vice President of the International University of the Caribbean.

Delores Gauntlett was born in St. Ann, Jamaica, in 1949. She is the author of *Freeing Her Hands to Clap* and *The Watertank Revisited* (Peepal Tree). Her poetry has appeared in the *Caribbean Writer*, *Poetry News*, *Kunapipi (Journal of Postcolonial Writing)*, *Observer Literary Arts*, *Jamaica Journal*, *Calabash Journal*, *Sunday Gleaner*, *New Caribbean Poetry*, and *Journal of Caribbean Literatures* among many others. Short-listed for the 2007 Hamish Canham Prize, her awards for poetry include the 1999 David Hough Prize and the 2006 *Daily News* Prize.

Susan Goffe was born in Kingston, Jamaica, in 1957. A teacher of English who has been out of the formal system for many years, she is a Calabash Writer's Workshop Fellow. She is the chairperson of the Kingston chapter of Jamaicans for Justice.

Lorna Goodison is a poet, short-story writer, memoirist and artist. She was born in Kingston in 1947, lives and works in Canada, but still has a home in Jamaica. She has published eleven collections of poems: *Tamarind Season*, *I Am Becoming My Mother*, *Heartease*, *Poems*, *Selected Poems*, *To Us, All Flowers Are Roses*, *Turn Thanks*, *Guinea Woman*, *Travelling Mercies*, *Controlling the Silver*, and *Goldengrove*. She has also published three collections of short stories, *Baby Mother and the King of Swords*, *Fool-Fool Rose Is Leaving Labour-in-Vain Savannah* and *By Love Possessed*. Her family memoir, *From Harvey River*, was published in 2008. In 1999, she was awarded the Musgrave Gold Medal by the Institute of Jamaica for her contributions to literature

Jean Goulbourne was born in St. Elizabeth, Jamaica, and received her education at the University of the West Indies, Mona. Her publications include the poetry collections *Actors in the Arena*, *Under the Sun*, and *Woman Song* (Peepal Tree), as well as the novel *Excavation* (Peepal Tree) and the short story collection *Parable of the Mangoes*. She has also authored the children's books *Freedom Come* and *Little Meeta*. A recipient of a James A. Michener Fellowship, she is now retired and lives in Cross Keys, Jamaica.

Millicent Graham was born in Kingston, Jamaica, in 1974. A Calabash Writer's Workshop Fellow, her first book of poems, *The Damp in Things*, was published by Peepal Tree in 2009. She lives in Kingston, Jamaica where she is a practising Information Architect with an MSc in Human Centred Computer Systems from the University of Sussex. Her second collection, *The Way Home* is due out in 2012.

Sally Henzell is an artist, poet, designer, and adventurer; she lives and works in Treasure Beach, Jamaica, where she created the world-renowned boutique hotel, Jake's.

Ishion Hutchinson was born in Port Antonio, Jamaica. He attended the University of the West Indies, Mona, and received his MFA from New York University. His work has appeared in the *LA Review*, *Callaloo*, the *Caribbean Review of Books*, *Guernica*, *Ploughshares*, and *The Common*. He is a Calabash Writer's Workshop Fellow, and his first collection, *Far District*, was published by Peepal Tree in 2010 and won the 2011 PEN/Joyce Osterweil Award for Poetry.

Danielle Jennings was born in Saint Andrew, Jamaica in 1983. A graduate of the University of the West Indies, she has taught in high school, worked for charity and currently is employed as a paralegal.

Linton Kwesi Johnson became only the second living poet and the first black poet to have his work included in Penguin's Modern Classics series. Born in the town of Chapelton, Jamaica, in 1952, he migrated to London in 1963. He attended Goldsmith's College, University of London, where he studied sociology. His books include *Inglan Is a Bitch* and *Selected Poems*. Johnson's first album, *Dread Beat an' Blood*, was released in 1978. Since then he has released fourteen more, including *LKJ: Live in Paris* in 2004. One year later he won a Silver Musgrave Medal from the Institute of Jamaica. Johnson has headed his own record label, LKJ Records, since 1981. He has worked in journalism and still tours around the world with the Dennis Bovell Dub Band.

Evan Jones was born in Portland, Jamaica, in 1927. He attended Haverford College and received his bachelor's degree from Wadham College in Oxford. He has taught at Wesleyan University and George School in Newtown, Pennsylvania. He wrote the scripts for the feature films *King & Country*, *Modesty Blaise*, *Funeral in Berlin*, *A Show of Force*, and the television documentary series *The Fight Against Slavery*. He is the author of two novels, *Stone Haven* and *Alonso and the Drug Baron*.

Jackie Lawrence is diversity strategist and the Program Director for 3Dreads and a Baldhead's Literary Series. She has received the

National Library of Poetry's Editor's Choice Award for her submission to the *River of Dreams* anthology. She has collaborated on two chapbooks and in 2006 she published her first chapbook, *Surrender*. Her new collection, *Invisible Visibility: On Being Black, Fat and a Woman*, is to be published soon.

Easton Lee was born in Wait-a-bit, Jamaica. A poet of Jamaican and Chinese descent, he now lives in Florida. A retired priest, he has published the poetry collections *From Behind the Counter*, *Heritage Call*, and *Encounters*. He has also written a short story collection, *Big Run 'Fraid (...and other village stories)*.

Ann-Margaret Lim is a fellow of the Calabash Writer's Workshop. She has been published in the *Caribbean Writer*, *Caribbean Quarterly*, the *Journal of Caribbean Literature*, the *Pittsburgh Quarterly*, and *Calabash: A Journal of Caribbean Literature*. In 2007, she received a highly recommended designation for a poetry manuscript from the National Book Development Council of Jamaica and won top prize for a short story in the 2007 WiSPA Literary Competition. Her first poetry publication, *The Festival of Wild Orchid*, is forthcoming from Peepal Tree Press.

Raymond Mair was born in Jamaica in 1935. His poems have appeared in a number of publications, including the *Sunday Observer*, the *Sunday Gleaner*, the *Caribbean Writer*, and in the anthologies *Focus*, *Bearing Witness 2* and *3*, *Caribbean Poem, and So Much Things to Say*. He has received the Jamaica Festival Award and the *Observer* Literary Award.

Rachel Manley was born in England, but brought to Jamaica at the age of two and raised by her grandparents, N.W. Manley and Edna Manley, the sculptor and energetic promotor of Jamaican arts. She was the daughter of Michael Manley. Although she currently describes herself a sometime a poet, she is the author of three important collections, *Prisms*, *Poems 2* and *A Light Left On* (Peepal Tree). She has made her reputation as a writer with a series of memoirs: *Drumblair: Memories of a Jamaican Childhood*, *Slipstream: A Daughter Remembers*, published in the UK as *In My Father's Shade*, and *Horses in Her Hair: A Granddaughter's Story*.

Mbala's artistic journey began with the Self Theatrical Movement in Spanish Town, Jamaica, continuing at the Edna Manley College for the Visual and Performing Arts, and in drama groups such as Sistren Theatre Collective, where he was a set and costume designer, graphic artist, and musician. He is a member of Akwaaba de Drummers, the acoustic quartet Naseberry Jazz, and, with flutist/saxophonist Hugh "Papi" Pape, the Papiumba Big Band – which, despite its name, is a duo. Mbala's work has been published in several anthologies including *Focus 83*, *Wheel and Come Again: An Anthology of Reggae Poetry*, and *Voiceprint*. He is a vice president of the Poetry Society of Jamaica, and his collection of poetry, *Light in a Book of Stone*, was published in the 2005 Calabash chapbook series.

Shara McCallum was born in Kingston, Jamaica. She earned her bachelor's degree from the University of Miami, a MFA from the University of Maryland, and her PhD from Binghamton University in Poetry and African American and Caribbean Literature. McCallum directs Bucknell University's Stadler Center for Poetry. She has published several collections of poetry including *Song of Thieves*, *This Strange Land*, and *The Water Between Us*, which won the 1998 Agnes Lynch Starett Prize. In 2011 her most recent book, *The Face of Water: New and Selected Poems*, was published by Peepal Tree. She was a recipient of a National Endowment for the Arts Fellowship for Poetry.

Earl McKenzie, born in St. Andrew, Jamaica, in 1943, was awarded the Institute of Jamaica's Silver Musgrave Medal in 2001 for his contribution to literature. He is the author of two short story collections, *A Boy Named Ossie* and *Two Roads to Mount Joyful*, and three collections of poetry, *Against Linearity*, *A Poet's House* , and *The Almond Leaf*, as well as one academic text, *Philosophy in the West Indian Novel*. McKenzie obtained his BA and MFA from Columbia University, and his PhD from the University of British Columbia. He is a retired professor from the University of the West Indies, Mona, where he taught philosophy.

Mark McMorris was born in Kingston, Jamaica, and attended the Excelsior School. He earned a bachelor's degree from Columbia University, and has a master's degree in creative writing (poetry) and a doctorate in comparative literature from Brown University. McMorris currently teaches at Georgetown University, and is the former director of its Lannan Center for Poetics and Social Practice. A two-time winner of the Contemporary Poetry Series Award from the University of Georgia Press, McMorris is the author of several books of poetry: *The Café at Light*, *The Blaze of the Poui*, *The Black Reeds*, and *Moth-Wings*. His most recent book, *Entrepôt*, was published in 2010 by Coffee House Press.

Kei Miller was born in Jamaica in 1978. He has been a Vera Rubin Fellow at the Yaddo Arts Colony in New York and an International Writing Fellow at the University of Iowa. His books of poetry are *Kingdom of Empty Bellies* and *There Is an Anger that Moves*. His books of fiction include the short story collection *The Fear of Stones*, which was short-listed for a regional Commonwealth Writers' Prize and *The Same Earth*. In 2010, his newest novel, *The Last Warner Woman*, was published as well as a new poetry collection, *A Light Song of Light*. Miller currently teaches creative writing at the University of Glasgow.

David Mills received his MFA in creative writing from New York University and a BA from Yale University. He has had poems published in *Ploughshares*, *Fence*, *Jubilat*, *Callaloo*, Harvard's *Transition Magazine*, *Brooklyn Rail*, *Hanging Loose Press* and *Rattapallax*. He has received fellowships from Breadloaf, New York Foundation for the Arts, Henry James Travel, Pan African Literary Forum, Cave Canem and BRIO. He is the recipient of the Chicago State University Langston Hughes Poetry Prize. His first book *The Dream Detective* was published in 2009 and was a small press bestseller.

Monica Minott is a chartered accountant. She received two awards in the Jamaican National Book Development Council's annual literary competitions for book-length collections of her poetry. She was awarded first prize in the inaugural Small Axe poetry competition. Her poems have been published in the *Caribbean Writer* and *Small Axe*.

Pamela Mordecai is a playwright, editor, fiction writer, and poet, she has published numerous textbooks, children's books, four collections of poetry, a collection of short fiction and, with Martin Mordecai, a reference work, *Culture and Customs of Jamaica*. Her children's play, *El Numero Uno*, premiered in Toronto in 2010. She has edited/co-edited ground-breaking anthologies including *Jamaica Woman, Her True-True Name* and *From Our Yard: Jamaican Poetry since Independence*. She was joint founder, with Martin Mordecai, of the Sandberry Press. Her awards include the Institute of Jamaica's Centenary Medal, the Victor Reid Award for Children's Literature, and the BURLA Award for contributions to Caribbean literature. She lives in Canada.

Mervyn Morris was born in Kingston, Jamaica, in 1937. He was on the staff of the University of the West Indies from 1966 until 2002, and is now Professor Emeritus of Creative Writing and West Indian Literature. His poetry collections are *The Pond*, *Shadowboxing*, *Examination Centre* (New Beacon Books), *On Holy Week* (Dangaroo Press) and *I been there, sort of: New and Selected Poems* (Carcanet Press).

Mutabaruka, born Allan Hope in 1952, is perhaps Jamaica's most famous living poet. He is also a recording artist and host of the *Cutting Edge*, a talk show on Irie FM. His collections of poetry include *Outcry*, *Sun and Moon*, *The Book: First Poems,* and *The Next Poems*. He emerged on the music scene in 1981 with the release of the single "Every Time a Ear de Soun". Alligator Records released *Check It!*, his first of many albums, in 1983.

Geoffrey Philp is the author of the children's books *Grandpa Sydney's Anancy Stories* and *Marcus and the Amazons*; a novel, *Benjamin, My Son*;

167

two collections of short stories, *Uncle Obadiah and the Alien* and *Who's Your Daddy? And Other Stories,* and six poetry collections, *Exodus and Other Poems, Florida Bound, Hurricane Center, Xango Music,* and *Twelve Poems and a Story for Christmas*. He teaches English and creative writing at Miami Dade College where he is the chair of the College Preparatory Department. His newest book of poetry, *Dub Wise*, was published in 2010 by Peepal Tree Press.

Janett Plummer also performs as Melted Demerara. She has been featured in the anthologies *RED*, *A Storm between Fingers,* and *Hand-made Fire*. She founded Inspired Word, a women's poetry organization which promotes poetry's therapeutic qualities for women and children. A multi slam award winner, she was a semi-finalist in the UK Slam championships and a finalist at the London Literature Festival short story slam. She is a member of Malika's Kitchen and Inspired Word writers, as well as writing and performing with the poetry & theatre company Thea Poets. Her pamphlet *Lifemarks* was published by Flipped Eye in 2009.

Velma Pollard has published poems and stories in regional and international journals and anthologies. She is the author of a novel, two collections of short fiction, and several books of poetry. Her novella, *Karl*, won the Casa de las Américas Prize in 1992; she was awarded a Silver Musgrave Medal in 2006. Pollard is a retired senior lecturer in language education at the University of the West Indies, Mona. Her major research interests have been the Creole languages of the Anglophone Caribbean, the language of Caribbean literature, and Caribbean women's writing. Her collection, *Considering Women 1 & 2: Short Stories*, was published in 2010 by Peepal Tree Press.

Claudia Rankine was born in Kingston, Jamaica. She is the author of four collections of poetry, *Don't Let Me Be Lonely*, *PLOT*, *The End of the Alphabet*, and *Nothing in Nature Is Private*, along with the play *The Provenance of Beauty: A South Bronx Travelogue*, produced in collaboration with the Foundry Theatre. She is also the co-editor of *American Women Poets in the Twenty-First Century: Where Lyric Meets Language* and

American Poets in the Twenty-First Century: The New Poetics. A recipient of fellowships from the Academy of American Poetry, the National Endowment for the Arts, and the Lannan Foundation, Rankin is the Henry G. Lee Professor of English at Pomona College.

Heather Royes' poems have been anthologized in the *Heinemann Book of Caribbean Poetry*, the *Penguin Book of Caribbean Verse*, the *Oxford Book of Caribbean Verse*, and *Seven Jamaican Women Writers*. In 2005 she published a collection of poetry, *Days and Nights of the Blue Iguana* (Peepal Tree). She has been awarded Silver and Bronze medals at the Jamaican Festival Literary Competition.

Saffron, born Phillippa Sauterel, is a Jamaican poet, porcelain artist, marketing graduate and realtor. She has performed her poetry regularly in prominent Kingston locations, and was featured as a special guest poet at the Poetry Society of Jamaica's fellowship in September 2001. She has appeared on the television programmes *Jamaica Magazine* and *Lyrically Speaking*, and her work has been published in the *Sunday Observer* and the anthologies *Bearing Witness 2 & 3* as well as *So Much Things To Say*. Her first collection of poetry, *Soft Flesh*, was published in the 2005 Calabash chapbook series.

Olive Senior's latest books are the novel *Dancing Lessons* and a children's picture book, *Birthday Suit*. She is the prizewinning author of twelve other books of fiction, poetry, and non-fiction, including Commonwealth Writers Prizewinning *Summer Lightning* and *Over the Roofs of the World*, which was a finalist for Canada's Governor-General's Award. She has also written *Shell*, a finalist for the Pat Lowther Award, *Gardening in the Tropics*, and the *Encyclopaedia of Jamaican Heritage*. She is a recipient of the Musgrave Gold Medal from the Institute of Jamaica. She conducts workshops internationally and lives in Toronto and Montego Bay.

Tanya Shirley lives in her native Jamaica. She received an MFA in creative writing from the University of Maryland, and is a graduate student and teacher in the Department of Literatures at the University of the West Indies, Mona. Her work has appeared in *Small Axe*, *Caribbean Writer*, and in *New Caribbean Poetry: An Anthology*. She is a Cave Canem Fellow and past participant in Callaloo creative writing workshops. Her first book of poems, *She Who Sleeps with Bones*, was published in 2009 by Peepal Tree Press.

A-dZiko Simba is a creative arts practitioner and consultant whose writing reflects her pan-Afrikanism. Her work, covering all creative genres from poetry to film scripts, has received numerous local and regional awards. Most recently she worked with Jamaica's Sistren Theatre Collective creating street theatre with two inner-city drama groups. She is currently working on a poetry collection, *Tales from the Pen*, and a series of children's books for Blue Moon Publishing.

Mary Lou Soutar-Hynes is a Jamaican-Canadian poet/educator and former nun with an interest in poetic inquiry. A 2009 Hawthornden Fellow, her publications include *Travelling Light* (2006), long-listed for the 2007 ReLit Poetry Award, and *The Fires of Naming* (2001) from Seraphim Editions, and poetry in journals and anthologies including *Calling Cards: New Poetry from Caribbean/Canadian Women* (2005), Sandberry Press and *Resonance: Poetry and Art* (2008), Sixth Floor Press. An essay, "Questionable Certainties," in *Canadian Woman Studies / les cahiers de la femme*, and chapter, "Points of Articulation," in *The Art of Poetic Inquiry*, Backalong Books are forthcoming in 2012.

Born in Kingston, **Andrew Stone** is a graduate of the University of the West Indies (Mona). His chapbook, *In Disguise*, was published by the Calabash Literary Trust and his work has appeared in several anthologies, locally and internationally. A consistent contributor to the literary arts output of the Sunday newspaper publications in Jamaica, Stone has also produced and presented "Lyrically Speaking", a television magazine programme focused on Jamaican and Caribbean writing.

fabian thomas is a Calabash Writers Workshop Fellow, whose work has appeared in *Sojourner: Black Gay Voices in the Age of AIDS* (1993), *Gents, Bad Boys & Barbarians: New Gay Male Poetry* (Alyson Books, 1995), *Fighting Words: Personal Essays by Black Gay Men* (Harper Collins, 1999), *Chroma: A Queer Literary Journal: Foreigners* (2005), *So Much Things To Say, 100 Calabash Poets* (Akashic Books) and *The Caribbean Writer*. In 2011 thomas was awarded the Charlotte & Isidor Paiewonsky Prize (for first time publication) by *The Caribbean Writer* for his poem "No One Helped Him".

Ralph Thompson has published poems in British, American, and Caribbean journals including the *Caribbean Writer* and the *Mississippi Review*. His work is represented in *The Heinemann Book of Caribbean Poetry*, *A World of Poetry* for CXC, several *Observer* art magazine anthologies, *The Oxford Book of Caribbean Verse*, and *Writers Who Paint/ Painters Who Write*. He has published two collections of poetry, *The Denting of a Wave* and *Moving On*, and a verse novel, *Views from Mount Diablo*, which won the Jamaican National Literary Prize for a manuscript in 2001. His *Taking Words for a Walk: New and Selected Poems* will be published by Peepal Tree in 2012.

Donna Aza Weir-Soley was born in Jamaica and received her PhD from the University of California, Berkeley. A recipient of the Woodrow Wilson Career Enhancement Fellowship, she has published the poetry collection, *First Rain* (Peepal Tree) and a book of literary criticism titled *Eroticism, Spirituality, and Resistance in Black Women's Writings*. She is an associate professor of English, African, and African Diaspora Studies at Florida International University. *Caribbean Erotic: Prose, Poetry & Essays*, an anthology she co-edited with Opal Palmer Adisa, was published in 2011.

d'bi.young is an Afrikan-Jamaican-Canadian dubpoet, monodramatist and educator who works with avant-garde, socially-conscious theatre in Canada. Young has published six plays, two collections of poetry, six dub poetry albums, and is anthologized in over 20 publications worldwide. Her work has included projects alongside Leonard Cohen, Djanet Sears, Margaret Atwood, k'naan, Oliver Mtukudzi, Harry Belafonte and Michael Ondaatje. She is the recipient of two Dora Mavor Moore awards, the Canadian K.M. Hunter theatre Award, the Toronto Mayor's Arts Council award, the Harold Award, and the Canadian Women's Resiliency Award. Young's monodrama trilogy *sankofa* was produced by Playwrights Canada Press and Tarragon Theatre.

ACKNOWLEDGMENTS

Opal Palmer Adisa, "Fire Eating Girl", © 2011. Used by permission of the author.

Lillian Allen, "Jamaica – I Remember", ©2011. Used by permission of the author.

Edward Baugh, "Yabba", © 2011. Used by permission of the author.

Jacqueline Bishop, "Recipe", previously published in *Snapshots from Istanbul*, © 2009, Peepal Tree Press. Used by permission of the author and publisher.

Jean "Binta" Breeze, "Third World Girl", previously published in *Third World Girl*. © 2011, Bloodaxe Books, Ltd. Used by permission of the author and publisher.

Frances Coke, "And Still I See", © 2011. Used by permission of the author.

Mel Cooke, "Country Come a Town", © 2011. Used by permission of the author.

Christine Craig, "My Son", © 2011. Used by permission of the author.

Kwame Dawes, "Impossible Flying" previously published in *Impossible Flying*, © 2007; "A Complex Ageless Longing" and "Upon Our Fourteenth Anniversary" in *Wheels*, © 2010, both Peepal Tree Press. Used by permission of the author and publisher.

Richard "Dingo" Dingwall, "In Third World's Shade", © 2011. Used by permission of the author.

Marcia Douglas, "Voice Lesson from the Unleashed Woman's Unabridged Dictionary" and "The Gift of Tongues", previously published in *Electricity Comes to Cocoa Bottom*, © 1999. Used by permission of the author and publisher.

Makesha Evans, "Different Revolutions" and "Where We…" © 2011. Used by permission of the author.

Delores Gauntlett, "Ponciana Tree In Bloom" and "To the Beat of the Tambourine", © 2011. Used by permission of the author.

Susan Goffe, "Still We Sing", © 2011. Used by permission of the author.

Lorna Goodison, "Hope Gardens", "Our Blessed Country Lady" and "Charlie Chaplin at Golden Clouds", © 2012. Used by permission of the author.

Jean Goulbourne, "Politician," previously published in *The Sunday Observer*, © 2011. Used by permission of the author.

173

175

ABOUT THE EDITOR

Born in Ghana in 1962, Kwame Dawes spent most of his childhood and early adult life in Jamaica. As a poet, he is profoundly influenced by its rhythms and textures, citing in a recent interview his "spiritual, intellectual, and emotional engagement with reggae music." His book, *Natural Mysticism*, explores that engagement.

He has published seventeen collections of poetry, two poetry anthologies, three works of fiction, four works of non-fiction and a play. His essays have appeared in numerous journals including *Bomb Magazine*, *The London Review of Books*, *Granta*, *Essence*, *World Literature Today* and *Double Take Magazine*.

A collection of his plays will come out in 2012.

Until July 2011, Dawes was Distinguished Poet in Residence, Louis Frye Scudder Professor of Liberal Arts and founder, and executive director of the South Carolina Poetry Initiative. He was the director of the University of South Carolina Arts Institute and is the programming director of the Calabash International Literary Festival, which takes place in Jamaica in May of each year. Dawes is currently the Glenna Luschei Editor of *Prairie Schooner* at the University of Nebraska, where he is a Chancellor's Professor of English, a faculty member of Cave Canem, and a teacher in the Pacific MFA Program in Oregon.

In 2009 he won an Emmy Award in the category New Approaches to News and Documentary Programming: Arts, Lifestyle and Culture for his work on www.LiveHopeLove.com, a multimedia website on the human face of HIV/AIDS in Jamaica. It was this project that inspired the collection *Hope's Hospice*, 2009. In 2012 he was honoured with the Barnes and Noble Writers for Writers Award and a Guggenheim Fellowship.

JAMAICAN TITLES FROM PEEPAL TREE

Opal Palmer Adisa, *Caribbean Passion*
ISBN: 9781900715928, Price: £7.99, poetry

Opal Palmer Adisa, *I Name Me Name*
ISBN: 9781845230449, Price: £9.99, poetry & essays

Opal Palmer Adisa, *Until Judgement Comes: Stories About Jamaican Men*
ISBN: 9781845230425, Price: £8.99, short stories

Opal Palmer Adisa, *Painting Away Regrets*
ISBN: 9781845230521, Price: £12.99, fiction

Jacqueline Bishop, *Fauna*
ISBN: 9781845230326, Price: £7.99, poetry

Jacqueline Bishop, *The River's Song*
ISBN: 9781845230388, Price: £8.99, fiction

Jacqueline Bishop, *Snapshots from Istanbul*
ISBN: 9781845231149, Price: £7.99, poetry

Jacqueline Bishop (ed.) *Writers Who Paint, Painters Who Write*
ISBN: 9781845230647, Price: £8.99, non-fiction

Lloyd W. Brown, *Duppies*
ISBN: 9780948833830, Price: £7.99, poetry

George Campbell, *First Poems*
ISBN: 9781845231491, Price: £9.99, poetry, classic

Hazel Campbell, *Singerman*
ISBN: 9780948833441, Price: £8.99, short stories

Frances Marie Coke, *Intersections*
ISBN: 9781845230884, Price: £7.99, poetry

Christine Craig, *All Things Bright & Quadrille for Tigers*
ISBN: 9781845231729, Price: £9.99, poetry

Kwame Dawes, *Progeny of Air*
ISBN: 9780948833687, Price: £7.99, poetry

Kwame Dawes, *Prophets*
ISBN: 9780948833854, Price: £7.99, poetry

Kwame Dawes, *Jacko Jacobus*
ISBN: 9781900715065, Price: £8.99, poetry

Kwame Dawes (ed.), *Shook Foil: a collection of reggae poetry*
ISBN: 9781900715140, Price: £7.99, poetry anthology

Kwame Dawes, *Natural Mysticism: Towards a new Reggae Aesthetic*
ISBN: 9781900715225, Price: £14.99, criticism

Kwame Dawes, *A Place to Hide*
ISBN: 9781900715485, Price: £9.99, short stories

Kwame Dawes, *A Far Cry from Plymouth Rock: A Personal Narrative*
ISBN: 9781845230258, Price: £12.99, memoir

Kwame Dawes, *New and Selected Poems*
ISBN: 9781900715706, Price: £9.99, poetry

Kwame Dawes, *Impossible Flying*
ISBN: 9781845230395, Price: £8.99, poetry

Kwame Dawes, *Back of Mount Peace*
ISBN: 9781845231248, Price: £8.99, poetry

Kwame Dawes, *Bivouac*
ISBN: 9781845231057, Price: £9.99, fiction

Kwame Dawes, *Hope's Hospice*
ISBN: 9781845230784, Price: £7.99, poetry

Neville Dawes, *Fugue and Other Writings*
ISBN: 9781845231095, Price: £9.99, poetry, short stories, criticism

Neville Dawes, *The Last Enchantment*
ISBN: 9781845231170, Price: £9.99, fiction

Marcia Douglas, *Electricity Comes To Cocoa Bottom*
ISBN: 9781900715287, Price: £7.99, poetry

Marcia Douglas, *Notes from a Writer's Book of Cures and Spells*
ISBN: 9781845230166, Price: £8.99, fiction

Gloria Escoffery, *Mother Jackson Murders the Moon*
ISBN: 9781900715249, Price: £7.99, poetry

John Figueroa, *The Chase*
ISBN: 9780948833526, Price: £9.99, poetry

Curdella Forbes, *A Permanent Freedom*
ISBN: 9781845230616, Price: £8.99, fiction

Curdella Forbes, *Ghosts*
ISBN: 9781845232009 Price: £9.99, fiction

Delores Gauntlett, *The Watertank Revisited*
ISBN: 9781845230098, Price: £7.99, poetry

Jean Goulbourne, *Woman Song*
ISBN: 9781900715034, Price: £7.99, poetry

Jean Goulbourne, *Excavation*
ISBN: 9781900715119, Price: £7.99, fiction

Millicent A. A. Graham, *The Damp in Things*
ISBN: 9781845230838, Price: £7.99, poetry

John Hearne, *Voices Under The Window*
ISBN: 9781845230319, Price: £7.99, fiction

Ishion Hutchinson, *Far District*
ISBN: 9781845231576, Price: £8.99, poetry

Clyde Knight, *Woman, Hold Your Head and Cry*
ISBN: 9780948833298, Price: £8.99, fiction

Roger Mais, *The Hills Were Joyful Together*
ISBN: 9781845231002, Price: £12.99, fiction, classic

Roger Mais, *Black Lightning*
ISBN: 9781845231019, Price: £9.99, fiction, classic

Rachel Manley, *A Light Left On*
ISBN: 9780948833557, Price: £7.99, poetry

Una Marson, *Selected Poems*
ISBN: 9781845231682, Price: £10.99, poetry, classic

Shara McCallum, *The Face of Water: New and Selected Poems*
ISBN: 9781845231866, Price: £9.99, poetry

Diana McCaulay, *Dog-Heart*
ISBN: 9781845231231, Price: £9.99, fiction

Diana McCaulay, *Huracan*
ISBN: 9781845231965, Price: £10.99, fiction

Alecia McKenzie, *Stories from Yard*
ISBN: 9781900715621, Price: £7.99, short stories

Alecia McKenzie, *Sweetheart*
ISBN: 9781845231774, Price: £8.99, fiction

Earl McKenzie, *Against Linearity*
ISBN: 9780948833632, Price: £7.99, poetry

Earl McKenzie, *The Almond Leaf*
ISBN: 9781845230128, Price: £7.99, poetry

Anthony McNeill, *Chinese Lanterns from the Blue Child*
ISBN: 9781900715188, Price: £7.99, poetry

Brian Meeks, *Paint the Town Red*
ISBN: 9781900715744, Price: £7.99, fiction

Orlando Patterson, *The Children of Sisyphus*
ISBN: 9781845230944, Price: £9.99, fiction, classic

Geoffrey Philp, *Florida Bound*
ISBN: 9780948833823, Price: £7.99, poetry

Geoffrey Philp, *Hurricane Center*
ISBN: 9781900715232, Price: £7.99, poetry

Geoffrey Philp, *Xango Music*
ISBN: 9781900715461, Price: £7.99, poetry

Geoffrey Philp, *Uncle Obadiah and the Alien*
ISBN: 9781900715010, Price: £7.99, short stories

Geoffrey Philp, *Benjamin, My Son*
ISBN: 9781900715782, Price: £8.99, fiction

Geoffrey Philp, *Who's Your Daddy? And Other Stories*
ISBN: 9781845230777, Price: £8.99, short stories

Geoffrey Philp, *Dub Wise*
ISBN: 9781845231712, Price: £8.99, poetry

Velma Pollard, *Crown Point*
ISBN: 9780948833243, Price: £7.99, poetry

Velma Pollard, *Shame Trees*
ISBN: 9780948833489, Price: £7.99, poetry

Velma Pollard, *Leaving Traces*
ISBN: 9781845230210, Price: £8.99, poetry

Velma Pollard, *Considering Woman I & II*
ISBN: 9781845231699, Price: £8.99, fiction

Patricia Powell, *The Fullness of Everything*
ISBN: 9781845231132, Price: £8.99, fiction

Victor Stafford Reid, *New Day*
ISBN: 9781845230906, Price: £13.99, fiction, classic

Heather Royes, *Days and Nights of the Blue Iguana*
ISBN: 9781845230197, Price: £7.99, poetry

Andrew Salkey, *Escape to An Autumn Pavement*
ISBN: 9781845230982, Price: £8.99, fiction, classic

Andrew Salkey, *Hurricane*
ISBN: 9781845231804, Price: £6.99, fiction, children's, classic

Andrew Salkey, *Drought*
ISBN: 9781845231835, Price: £6.99, fiction, children's, classic

Andrew Salkey, *Earthquake*
ISBN: 9781845231828, Price: £6.99, fiction, children's, classic

Andrew Salkey, *Riot*
ISBN: 9871845231819, Price: £7.99, fiction, children's, classic

Dennis Scott, *After-Image*
ISBN: 9781845230241, Price: £7.99, poetry

Verene Shepherd, *Transients to Settlers: The Experience of Indians in Jamaica*
ISBN: 9780948833328, Price: £12.99, history

Tanya Shirley, *She Who Sleeps With Bones*
ISBN: 9781845230876, Price: £7.99, poetry

Ralph Thompson, *The Denting of a Wave*
ISBN: 9780948833625, Price: £7.99, poetry

Ralph Thompson, *Moving On*
ISBN: 9781900715171, Price: £8.99, poetry

Ralph Thompson, *View from Mount Diablo, annotated edition*
ISBN: 9781845231446, Price: £12.99, poetry

Ralph Thompson, *Taking Words for a Walk*
ISBN: 9781845231958, Price: £9.99, poetry

Donna Aza Weir-Solcy, *First Rain*
ISBN: 9781845230333, Price: £7.99, poetry

Gwyneth Barber Wood, *The Garden of Forgetting*
ISBN: 9781845230074, Price: £7.99, poetry

All Peepal Tree titles are available from the website
www.peepaltreepress.com
Contact us at:
Peepal Tree Press, 17 King's Avenue, Leeds LS6 1QS, UK
Tel: +44 (0) 113 2451703 E-mail: contact@peepaltreepress.com